Better Homes and Gardens®

Vegetarian
COOKING

Better Homes and Gardens® Books
Des Moines, Iowa

All of us at Better Homes and Gardens® Books are dedicated to providing you with the information and ideas you need to create delicious foods. We welcome your comments and suggestions. Write to us at Better Homes and Gardens Books, Cookbook Editorial Department, 1716 Locust St., Des Moines, IA 50309-3023.

If you would like to purchase any of our cooking, crafts, gardening, home improvement, or home decorating and design books, check wherever quality books are sold. Or visit us at: bhgbooks.com.

Our seal assures you that every recipe in *Vegetarian Cooking* has been tested in the Better Homes and Gardens® Test Kitchen. This means that each recipe is practical and reliable, and meets our high standards of taste appeal. We guarantee your satisfaction with this book for as long as you own it.

Pictured on front cover:
Trattoria-Style Fettucine, page 74

Cover Photo:
Pete Krumhardt, Photographer;
Dianna Nolin, Food Stylist

Better Homes and Gardens® Books
An imprint of Meredith® Books

Vegetarian Cooking
Editor: Chuck Smothermon
Associate Art Director: Lynda Haupert
Copy Chief: Terri Fredrickson
Editorial Operations Manager: Karen Schirm
Managers, Book Production: Pam Kvitne, Marjorie J. Schenkelberg
Recipe Developers: Ellen Boeke, Marcia Stanley
Contributing Copy Editor: Donna Segal
Contributing Proofreaders: Maria Duryee, Gretchen Kauffman, Susan J. Kling
Indexer: Elizabeth Parson
Electronic Production Coordinator: Paula Forest
Editorial and Design Assistants: Judy Bailey, Mary Lee Gavin
Test Kitchen Director: Lynn Blanchard
Test Kitchen Product Supervisor: Marilyn Cornelius
Test Kitchen Home Economists: Judy Comstock, Jennifer Kalinowski, R.D., Maryellyn Krantz, Jill Lust, Jill Moberly, Kay Springer, Colleen Weeden, Lori Wilson

Meredith® Books
Editor in Chief: James D. Blume
Design Director: Matt Strelecki
Managing Editor: Gregory H. Kayko
Executive Food Editor: Jennifer Dorland Darling

Director, Sales, Special Markets: Rita McMullen
Director, Sales, Premiums: Michael A. Peterson
Director, Sales, Retail: Tom Wierzbicki
Director, Book Marketing: Brad Elmitt
Director, Operations: George A. Susral
Director, Production: Douglas M. Johnston

Better Homes and Gardens® Magazine
Editor in Chief: Karol De Wulf Nickell

Meredith Publishing Group
President, Publishing Group: Stephen M. Lacy

Meredith Corporation
Chairman and Chief Executive Officer: William T. Kerr

Chairman of the Executive Committee: E. T. Meredith III

Contents

Welcome to Our Kitchen

When you cook with a Better Homes and Gardens® cookbook, you can be confident that every recipe will taste great every time. That's because we perfect every recipe in our Test Kitchen before we present it to you.

The Home Economists in the Better Homes and Gardens® Test Kitchen have enthusiastically developed thousands of meatless main-dish recipes over the years. Never have we been more excited about the possibilities for creating wholesome and infinitely interesting vegetarian meals.

Timing is everything. As dietitians continue to learn more about ways vegetarian meals can fit into a low-fat, high-fiber, vitamin-rich diet, markets everywhere are brimming with fresh and lively ingredients that make meatless dining more varied and satisfying than ever.

We loved working with this world of great ingredients to create fresh, innovative, up-to-date recipes, many with enticing ethnic touches. And we're equally fond of giving popular comfort foods—such as cassoulet, Hoppin' John, and chowder—thoroughly vegetarian angles. So whether you're in the mood for something worldly or homey (or a little bit of both), chances are you'll find just what you're looking for in this book.

Of course, our vegetarian recipes go through all the rigorous standards of testing and tasting that any of our recipes do. We have a vegetarian on staff who's familiar with the latest and greatest trends in vegetarian dining; we also have many meat-eaters on staff—and they wouldn't let a recipe pass through our taste panel if it wasn't wholly satisfying. I'm confident that the only thing missing in these recipes is the meat. So go ahead! Go meatless—every day or now and then. With these recipes, I'm sure you'll enjoy it as much as we did.

Lynn Blanchard

Lynn Blanchard
Better Homes and Gardens®
Test Kitchen Director

Vegetarian Q&A

Whether you go meatless every day or once in a while, read on! Answers to these frequently asked questions will help you discover more about the healthful world of vegetarian-style eating.

Q.

What are the health benefits of vegetarian dining?

A.

In short, health authorities recommend a low-fat, high-fiber, vitamin-rich diet, and vegetarian-style eating can help you and your family attain these goals.

More specifically, the abundance of fruits, vegetables, legumes, and grains in vegetarian diets provides vitamins, minerals, and fiber the body needs. Moreover, they contain certain compounds, called phytochemicals, that are believed to help fend off heart disease and cancer.

Also, according to the American Dietetic Association, vegetarians—especially vegans (see definition, page 16)—have lower mortality rates from such chronic diseases and conditions as heart disease, hypertension, certain cancers, diabetes, and obesity. Of course, other healthful lifestyle choices that vegetarians often make (such as frequent exercising and not smoking) can play a beneficial role too.

Q.

Are all vegetarian diets healthful?

A.

A vegetarian diet does not necessarily ensure a healthy diet. Like everyone else, vegetarians need to keep an eye on fat, calories, and cholesterol (especially if cheese, eggs, and/or dairy products are on the menu). Meal planning requires special attention; vegans, in particular, need to ensure that their menu provides plenty of calories and a variety of nutrients.

Q.

Can I supplement my diet with vitamin supplements?

A.

Before taking vitamin supplements, talk to your doctor or a registered dietitian (R.D.) for guidelines. Keep in mind that high dosages of some nutrients, including vitamin D, vitamin B_{12}, and zinc, can be dangerous; therefore, you should avoid supplements that exceed your Recommended Daily Allowance (RDA) of such nutrients per day.

Q.

Is it possible to get enough protein in a vegetarian diet?

A.

Many plant foods (with the exception of fruit) are rich in protein, so for most vegetarians getting enough protein isn't an issue. It's important each day to eat a variety of foods that contain protein.

The nutrients more likely to be lacking in a vegetarian diet include vitamin B_{12}, vitamin D, calcium, iron, and zinc. Good vegetarian sources of these nutrients are:

● **Vitamin B_{12}:** Breakfast cereals, soymilk products, and vegetarian burger patties fortified with vitamin B_{12}. Getting enough B_{12} is generally not a concern for vegetarians who eat dairy products or eggs.

● **Vitamin D:** Milk is naturally high in vitamin D; vegans should look for breakfast cereals and soy beverages fortified with the nutrient.

● **Calcium:** If you regularly consume milk, cheese, and yogurt, your calcium intake should be adequate. Those avoiding dairy products can opt for green leafy vegetables, calcium-fortified orange juice, and fortified soymilk and soy cheese.

● **Iron:** Reach for legumes, dark-green leafy vegetables, iron-fortified cereals and bread, whole-grain products, seeds, prune juice, dried fruit, and black-strap molasses. Keep in mind that eating a vitamin C-rich food at every meal will help your body absorb the type of iron that's found in plant sources.

● **Zinc:** Whole grains, especially germ and bran (note that grains processed into refined flour lose zinc), whole-wheat bread, legumes, tofu, seeds, and nuts are good sources for zinc.

Q.

What health issues do parents need to consider if their children are vegetarians?

A.

Because vegetarian meals are often low in fat and high in fiber, they might not supply kids with the calories needed to fuel their growing bodies. Offering your child higher calorie foods, along with foods with more fat such as peanut butter, nuts, and cheese can help meet these needs. Also, encourage frequent snacks that provide both calories and needed nutrients—a peanut butter sandwich and milk, for example.

While vegetarian children who consume dairy and eggs can generally get the nutrients they need, vegan youngsters, from infants to teens, may have difficulty obtaining adequate amounts of vitamin B_{12}, vitamin D, calcium, iron, and zinc. If your child is a vegan, make sure he or she gets adequate amounts of these nutrients through a variety of foods.

You should also obtain nutrition counseling for your vegetarian child from a registered dietitian, doctor, or a pediatric nurse. Ask for their recommendations on nutritional supplements.

Appetizers

Spicy Tofu Triangles

In this Chapter:

♥ Low-fat and no-fat recipes
✳ Fast recipes

Curry-Chutney Dip

A little bit nutty, a little bit spicy, this intriguing Indian-inspired recipe journeys off the well-beaten chip-and-dip path. Choose a chutney to suit your taste—some are sweeter, others are hot.

Prep: 10 minutes **Chill:** 2 hours **Makes:** Ten 2-tablespoon servings

¼ cup mango chutney
½ of an 8-ounce package
    reduced-fat cream
    cheese (Neufchâtel),
    softened
⅔ cup light dairy sour cream
1 teaspoon curry powder
¼ cup chopped dry roasted
    or honey-roasted
    cashews
    Crisp breadsticks and/or
    assorted vegetable
    dippers

1 Snip any large pieces in chutney; set aside. In a small bowl stir together cream cheese, sour cream, and curry powder. Stir in chutney. Cover and refrigerate for 2 to 48 hours.

2 Before serving, sprinkle the dip with cashews. Serve with breadsticks and/or vegetables.

Nutrition Facts per 2 tablespoons dip: 92 cal., 6 g total fat (3 g sat. fat), 14 mg chol., 84 mg sodium, 8 g carbo., 0 g fiber, 3 g pro.
Daily Values: 10% vit. A, 5% vit. C, 4% calcium, 2% iron
Exchanges: ½ Starch, 1 Fat

chutneys

Chutneys, generally made from fruit, sugar, spices, and vinegar, can be chunky or smooth and hot or mildly hot. They are best known for being a partner to Indian curry dishes. With the many combinations of fruit and spices that are possible, chutneys also can be used as a jam to spread on bread, or served with cheese and crackers.

Saffron Potato Omelet Tapas

Stateside, omelets aren't thought of as appetizer fare. Yet, in the taverns of Spain, they serve small portions of these potato-filled rounds as part of an informal tapas spread.

Prep: 15 minutes **Cook:** 12 minutes **Stand:** 10 minutes **Makes:** 8 to 10 servings

½ cup olive oil or cooking oil
1¼ pounds white potatoes, peeled and thinly sliced (3 cups)
1 medium onion, thinly sliced
4 eggs
¼ teaspoon salt
Pinch thread saffron, crushed

1 In a large nonstick skillet heat oil over medium-high heat. Add potatoes and onion; reduce heat to medium. Cook, covered, for 8 to 10 minutes or just until potatoes are tender, gently stirring occasionally. Drain potato mixture, reserving oil. Wipe out skillet with paper towels.

2 In a large bowl beat together eggs, salt, and saffron until slightly frothy. Add potato mixture. Gently press down potatoes with a spatula to moisten with egg mixture. Let stand for 10 minutes.

3 In the same skillet heat 1 tablespoon of the reserved oil over medium-high heat; lift and tilt the skillet until the oil coats bottom and sides. Add egg mixture all at once; reduce heat to medium. Cook for 2 to 3 minutes or until eggs are brown and set on bottom, shaking skillet often to prevent sticking (some uncooked egg mixture will remain on top).

4 Loosen omelet from sides of skillet; place a large inverted plate over skillet. Invert and lift off the skillet. Slide the omelet back into skillet. Cook for 2 to 3 minutes more or until eggs are brown on bottom. Slide omelet onto a serving plate. Cut into wedges and serve warm.

Nutrition Facts per serving: 152 cal., 9 g total fat (2 g sat. fat), 106 mg chol., 106 mg sodium, 12 g carbo., 1 g fiber, 5 g pro.
Daily Values: 3% vit. A, 17% vit. C, 2% calcium, 5% iron
Exchanges: 1 Starch, ½ Medium-Fat Meat, 1 Fat

Artichoke-Stuffed New Potatoes

Two popular contemporary appetizers—hot artichoke dip and stuffed potato skins—come together in one great nibble. New potatoes and a sprightly gremolata update this dynamic duo.

Prep: 25 minutes **Bake:** 20 minutes **Makes:** 16 appetizers

16 tiny new potatoes
      (1½ to 2 inch diameter)
 1 tablespoon olive oil
 1 14-ounce can artichoke
      hearts, drained and
      chopped
 ½ cup light mayonnaise
      dressing or salad
      dressing
 ¼ cup finely shredded
      Parmesan cheese
      Dash ground red pepper
 1 recipe Gremolata

1 Cut off the top one-third of each potato. Using a melon baller, hollow out the potatoes, leaving ¼-inch shells. Cut a thin slice off the bottom of each potato so it will sit without tipping. (Discard potato trimmings, or cook and use to make potato salad or mashed potatoes.) Lightly brush potatoes all over with oil. Place in a shallow baking pan; set aside.

2 For filling, in a medium bowl combine the artichoke hearts, mayonnaise dressing, Parmesan cheese, and ground red pepper. Spoon about 1 tablespoon of the filling into each potato shell.

3 Bake in a 450° oven about 20 minutes or until potatoes are tender and filling is golden brown. Sprinkle the gremolata over the potatoes.

Gremolata: In a small bowl combine ¼ cup snipped fresh parsley, 2 tablespoons finely shredded lemon peel, and 2 cloves minced garlic.

Nutrition Facts per potato: 70 cal., 4 g total fat (1 g sat. fat), 4 mg chol., 144 mg sodium, 7 g carbo., 1 g fiber, 2 g pro.
Daily Values: 2% vit. A, 12% vit. C, 3% calcium, 5% iron
Exchanges: ½ Starch, ½ Fat

Figgy Cheese Conserve FAST

Goat cheese and figs are a heavenly match, so go ahead and get figgy! As for something to drink, Sancerre or Riesling will complement this starter nicely.

Start to finish: 30 minutes **Makes:** 8 servings

8 dried figs
1 tablespoon margarine or butter
1 large onion, thinly sliced
1 teaspoon snipped fresh thyme
1 tablespoon balsamic vinegar
6 ounces soft goat cheese (chèvre)
   Assorted crackers (such as water crackers, pepper-flavored crackers, or stone-ground wheat crackers)

1 If desired, remove stems from figs. Halve or quarter figs. Place figs in a medium saucepan and cover with water. Bring to boiling; reduce heat. Simmer, covered, for 5 minutes. Drain and cool slightly.

2 In a medium skillet melt margarine over medium heat. Add onion; cook and stir about 5 minutes or until brown. Stir in figs and thyme. Cook about 2 minutes or until figs and onion are slightly softened, stirring gently. Stir in balsamic vinegar. Cook for 2 to 3 minutes more or until figs and onion are glazed, stirring occasionally.

3 To serve, place the fig mixture and the goat cheese in a serving bowl. Serve with crackers.

Nutrition Facts per serving of conserve: 183 cal., 7 g total fat (3 g sat. fat), 10 mg chol., 177 mg sodium, 25 g carbo., 3 g fiber, 6 g pro.
Daily Values: 2% vit. A, 3% vit. C, 6% calcium, 5% iron
Exchanges: ½ Fruit, 1 Starch, ½ High-Fat Meat, ½ Fat

Baby Vegetable Platter FAST

Baby vegetables are so beautiful, tender, and sweet, they don't need much preparation to get them ready for a party. This fresh and simple dip allows their rare qualities to star.

Start to finish: 30 minutes Makes: 10 to 12 servings

1 8-ounce loaf baguette-style French bread, cut into $\frac{1}{4}$-inch slices
2 tablespoons olive oil
2 tablespoons butter or margarine
$\frac{1}{4}$ cup finely chopped shallots
2 tablespoons all-purpose flour
$\frac{1}{8}$ teaspoon salt
   Dash black pepper
$\frac{1}{4}$ cup dry white wine
$\frac{3}{4}$ cup half-and-half or light cream
1 teaspoon snipped fresh thyme or $\frac{1}{4}$ teaspoon dried thyme, crushed
$4\frac{1}{2}$ ounces Brie cheese, rind removed and cut into $\frac{1}{2}$-inch pieces
   Assorted steamed baby vegetables (such as artichokes, carrots, summer squash, and/or green beans)

1 Lightly brush both sides of bread slices with oil. Place bread slices on a large baking sheet. Bake in a 400° oven for 6 to 8 minutes or until lightly browned. Set aside.

2 Meanwhile, in a small saucepan melt butter over medium heat. Add shallots; cook and stir about 3 minutes or until tender. Stir in flour, salt, and black pepper. Add wine all at once. Cook and stir for 1 minute. Add half-and-half and, if using, dried thyme. Cook and stir until thickened and bubbly. Cook and stir for 1 minute more. Reduce heat to low.

3 Add Brie cheese to wine mixture; stir until cheese is melted. If using, stir in fresh thyme. Transfer to a serving bowl. Serve warm with toasted bread slices and steamed baby vegetables.

Nutrition Facts per serving: 100 cal., 8 g total fat (5 g sat. fat), 26 mg chol., 141 mg sodium, 3 g carbo., 0 g fiber, 3 g pro.
Daily Values: 7% vit. A, 1% vit. C, 5% calcium, 1% iron
Exchanges: $\frac{1}{2}$ Medium-Fat Meat, $1\frac{1}{2}$ Fat

Spicy Tofu Triangles ♥

Vegetarians prize tofu as a champion of versatility—it melds perfectly with so many flavors and cooking styles. It's right at home wrapped into wonton skins with intriguing Asian ingredients.

Prep: 50 minutes **Bake:** 10 minutes **Makes:** 48 triangles

1 12-ounce package extra-firm, tub-style tofu (fresh bean curd), chopped

½ cup finely chopped fresh shiitake or button mushrooms

⅓ cup thinly sliced green onions

¼ cup finely chopped canned water chestnuts

2 tablespoons bottled hoisin sauce

2 teaspoons Oriental chili sauce with garlic

1 teaspoon soy sauce

48 wonton wrappers
    Nonstick cooking spray
    Teriyaki sauce and/or prepared Chinese-style hot mustard (optional)

1 For filling, in a large bowl combine tofu, mushrooms, green onions, water chestnuts, hoisin sauce, chili sauce, and soy sauce. Spoon about 1 tablespoon of the filling into the center of each wonton wrapper. Brush edges of wrapper with water. Fold one corner of wrapper to opposite corner to form a triangle; press edges to seal.

2 Lightly coat large baking sheets with cooking spray. Place the wonton triangles on prepared baking sheets. Lightly coat the triangles with cooking spray.

3 Bake in a 400° oven about 10 minutes or until triangles are crisp and golden brown. Drain on paper towels. If desired, serve the hot triangles with teriyaki sauce and/or mustard.

Nutrition Facts per triangle: 32 cal., 0 g total fat (0 g sat. fat), 1 mg chol., 67 mg sodium, 6 g carbo., 0 g fiber, 1 g pro.
Daily Values: 2% calcium, 2% iron
Exchanges: ½ Starch

Endive-Mango Appetizers ♥ FAST

Although these make a stunning appetizer, you also could serve a few endives filled with cream cheese and macadamia nuts as a side salad.

Start to finish: 20 minutes **Makes:** about 24 appetizers

1   3-ounce package cream cheese, softened

¼   cup coarsely chopped macadamia nuts

2   to 3 medium Belgian endives, separated into individual leaves

1   large mango or papaya, peeled and cut into thin strips

1 In a small bowl combine the cream cheese and macadamia nuts. Spread about 1 teaspoon of the cream cheese mixture onto each endive leaf.* Top with the mango strips. Arrange on a serving platter.

Nutrition Facts per appetizer: 29 cal., 2 g total fat (1 g sat. fat), 4 mg chol., 11 mg sodium, 2 g carbo., 0 g fiber, 0 g pro.
Daily Values: 5% vit. A, 5% vit. C
Exchanges: ½ Fat

*Note: You may cover loosely with plastic wrap and refrigerate up to 2 hours. Before serving, top with the mango strips.

managing a mango

Removing the large seed of a mango takes a little cutting expertise. First, I place the fruit on its blossom end and align a sharp knife slightly off-center on the stem end of the fruit. Then I slice down through the peel and flesh, next to the pit. I repeat the process on the other side of the seed and cut off the remaining flesh around the seed. Finally, I remove the peel and cut the mango into pieces as directed in the recipe I'm preparing.

Colleen Weeden

Test Kitchen Home Economist

Blue Cheese-Walnut Wafers

Simplicity is what makes these appetizers so appealing—they are easy to make and don't need a dip or spread to be wonderful.

Prep: 25 minutes **Bake:** 8 minutes **Chill:** 2 hours **Makes:** about 72 wafers

1½ cups all-purpose flour
2 to 3 teaspoons cracked black pepper
8 ounces blue cheese
¼ cup butter
1 cup chopped walnuts
2 slightly beaten egg yolks

1 In a medium bowl stir together flour and black pepper. Using a pastry blender, cut in blue cheese and butter until mixture resembles coarse crumbs. Add the walnuts and egg yolks; stir until combined. Shape mixture into a ball; knead until smooth.

2 Divide dough in half. Shape each half into a 9-inch-long log. Wrap logs in plastic wrap and refrigerate at least 2 hours.

3 Cut each log into ¼-inch slices. Place slices, about 1 inch apart, on ungreased large baking sheets. Bake in a 425° oven for 8 to 10 minutes or until bottoms and edges are golden brown. Transfer to wire racks. Serve warm or at room temperature. To store, cool completely. Place in a covered container and refrigerate up to 1 week.

Nutrition Facts per wafer: 38 cal., 3 g total fat (1 g sat. fat), 11 mg chol., 64 mg sodium, 2 g carbo., 0 g fiber, 1 g pro.
Daily Values: 2% vit. A, 1% calcium, 1% iron
Exchanges: ½ Fat

what is a vegetarian?

Broadly speaking, a vegetarian is one who doesn't eat meat, poultry, or fish. However, there are many types of vegetarians (including vegans) who have more specific parameters regarding their diets. Definitions for today's common categories of vegetarians:

- **Vegans** eat only foods that are plant based. This means they consume no meat, poultry, or fish, nor animal products such as milk, cheese, butter, and eggs.
- **Lacto-Vegetarians** are vegetarians who include dairy products in their diets, but no eggs.
- **Lacto-Ovo Vegetarians** include both dairy products and eggs in their diets.
- **Pollo-Vegetarians** include poultry in their diets.
- **Pesca-Vegetarians** include fish and other seafood in the diet.
- **The sometimes vegetarian** chooses mainly a plant-centered diet, with small amounts of animal-derived products consumed less frequently.

Herb and Pepper Lentil Stew

Soups

In this Chapter:

♥ Low-fat and no-fat recipes
* Fast recipes

Vegetable Stock ♥

So many soups are meatless—except when they call for chicken broth. Vegetarians will enjoy having this tasty alternative, as will anyone who wants to add a robust vegetable flavor to soup recipes.

Prep: 30 minutes **Cook:** 2 hours **Makes:** about 7 cups

4	medium onions
4	medium carrots
3	medium potatoes
2	medium parsnips, turnips, or rutabagas
1	small head cabbage
1	tablespoon olive oil
8	cups water
1	teaspoon salt
½	teaspoon dried dillweed or dried basil, rosemary, or marjoram, crushed
¼	teaspoon black pepper

1 Scrub all vegetables; cut off root and stem ends. Do not peel vegetables, unless coated with wax. Cut onions into wedges. Cut carrots, potatoes, parsnips, and cabbage into 2-inch pieces.

2 In a 6-quart Dutch oven heat oil over medium heat. Add vegetables. Cook about 10 minutes or until vegetables are starting to brown, stirring frequently. Stir in the water, salt, desired herb, and black pepper. Bring to boiling; reduce heat. Simmer, covered, for 2 hours.

3 To strain the stock, line a large colander with 2 layers of 100-percent-cotton cheesecloth. Set the colander in a large heatproof bowl or container. Ladle or pour the stock through the lined colander. Discard vegetables and seasonings.

4 To store, ladle or pour stock into a container, cover, and refrigerate up to 3 days or freeze up to 6 months.

Nutrition Facts per cup: 17 cal., 2 g total fat (0 g sat. fat), 0 mg chol.,
341 mg sodium, 0 g carbo., 0 g fiber, 0 g pro.
Daily Values: 1% calcium, 1% iron
Exchanges: ½ Fat

homemade vs. store bought

Although it may not pay to make some things yourself, stock may be worth the effort. If you have an overabundance of vegetables in your garden, making vegetable stock can save your garden from being wasted. Better yet, you don't have to use picture-perfect vegetables. Homemade stock also saves you about half the sodium of canned stock. So if you're watching your sodium intake or you have a bountiful garden that's a bit past its prime, making vegetable stock from scratch makes sense. Best of all, you control the types of vegetables that go into your stock that is a base for soups and other stock- or broth-based dishes.

Roasted Garlic Barley Soup ♥

A head of garlic may sound like a lot—but roasting it makes it oh-so mellow and sweet. Try this soup alongside Eggplant Panini (page 85) for a special weekend lunch.

Prep: 40 minutes **Cook:** 20 minutes **Makes:** 4 servings

1   medium head garlic
1   teaspoon olive oil or
      cooking oil
4   cups Vegetable Stock
      (recipe, page 18) or
      canned vegetable broth
1½ cups thinly sliced leeks
¾   cup thinly sliced celery
1½ teaspoons dried basil,
      crushed
⅛   teaspoon black pepper
1   14½-ounce can tomatoes,
      undrained and cut up
1   medium zucchini or
      yellow summer squash,
      halved lengthwise and
      thinly sliced
½   cup quick-cooking barley

1 Peel away the outer dry leaves from head of garlic, leaving skin of garlic cloves intact. Using a knife, cut off about ¼ inch of the pointed top portion of head, leaving the bulb intact but exposing individual cloves.

2 Place garlic head, cut side up, in a small baking dish; drizzle with oil. Bake, covered, in a 400° oven for 25 to 35 minutes or until cloves feel soft when pressed. Cool slightly. Press garlic pulp from individual cloves; mash pulp with a fork.

3 In a large saucepan combine the mashed garlic pulp, Vegetable Stock, leeks, celery, basil, and black pepper. Bring to boiling; reduce heat. Simmer, covered, about 10 minutes or until leeks and celery are tender.

4 Stir in the tomatoes, zucchini, and barley. Return to boiling; reduce heat. Simmer, covered, about 10 minutes more or until barley is tender.

Nutrition Facts per serving: 153 cal., 4 g total fat (1 g sat. fat), 0 mg chol., 557 mg sodium, 28 g carbo., 5 g fiber, 4 g pro.
Daily Values: 3% vit. A, 35% vit. C, 7% calcium, 12% iron
Exchanges: 2 Vegetable, 1 Starch, 1 Fat

Root Vegetable Soup ♥

Serve this hearty soup with a country-style bread and a selection of artisan cheeses for a rustic and comforting Sunday supper.

Prep: 20 minutes **Cook:** 25 minutes **Makes:** 4 to 6 servings

3½ cups Vegetable Stock (recipe, page 18) or two 14½-ounce cans vegetable broth

2 medium leeks, halved lengthwise and cut into 1- to 2-inch pieces

1 medium rutabaga, peeled and cut into 1-inch pieces

1 medium turnip, peeled and cut into 1-inch pieces

6 baby carrots, peeled, or 2 small carrots, peeled and cut up

1 small parsnip, peeled and cut up

½ cup dry sherry, Vegetable Stock, or canned vegetable broth

1 4-inch sprig fresh rosemary or ½ teaspoon dried rosemary, crushed

Fresh rosemary (optional)

1 In a 4-quart Dutch oven combine the Vegetable Stock, 2½ cups water, leeks, rutabaga, turnip, carrots, parsnip, sherry, and rosemary.

2 Bring to boiling; reduce heat. Simmer, uncovered, for 25 to 30 minutes or until rutabaga and turnip are tender. Discard rosemary sprig. If desired, garnish with additional fresh rosemary.

Nutrition Facts per serving: 112 cal., 2 g total fat (0 g sat. fat), 0 mg chol., 344 mg sodium, 15 g carbo., 3 g fiber, 2 g pro.
Daily Values: 121% vit. A, 29% vit. C, 6% calcium, 6% iron
Exchanges: 2 Vegetable, ½ Starch, ½ Fat

cleaning leeks

The tightly packed leaves of leeks taste delicious but easily collect soil. Properly cleaning them is a must. First remove any outer leaves that have wilted. Slice the leek lengthwise in half, all the way through the root end. Holding the leek under a faucet with the root end up, rinse the leek under cold running water, lifting and separating the leaves with your fingers to allow the grit to flow down through the top of the leek. Continue rinsing until all grit is removed. Slice off the root end before using.

Thai Lime Custard Soup ♥ FAST

With spiciness from the garlic and ginger, the peppery flavor of basil, and a spark of lime, this dish gathers a spectrum of Thai flavors into one beautiful bowl.

Start to finish: 25 minutes **Makes:** 5 servings

2 baby eggplants or
   Japanese eggplants
   (1 pound total), halved
   lengthwise and sliced
1 tablespoon grated fresh
   ginger
2 or 3 cloves garlic, minced
   (optional)
¼ teaspoon crushed red
   pepper
1 tablespoon cooking oil
3½ cups Vegetable Stock
   (recipe, page 18) or
   two 14½-ounce cans
   vegetable broth
3 eggs
2 cups chopped spinach
¼ cup finely shredded fresh
   basil
¼ cup lime juice

1 In a large saucepan cook eggplants, ginger, garlic (if desired), and crushed red pepper in hot oil over medium-high heat for 2 minutes. Add Vegetable Stock. Bring to boiling; reduce heat. Simmer, covered, for 5 minutes.

2 In a small bowl beat eggs with a fork. Gradually stir about ½ cup of the hot stock mixture into eggs. Return egg mixture to the remaining stock mixture. Add spinach.

3 Cook and stir over medium-low heat about 2 minutes or until soup is slightly thickened and spinach is wilted. Stir in basil and lime juice; heat through.

Nutrition Facts per serving: 109 cal., 7 g total fat (2 g sat. fat), 128 mg chol., 294 mg sodium, 7 g carbo., 3 g fiber, 5 g pro.
Daily Values: 21% vit. A, 14% vit. C, 4% calcium, 9% iron
Exchanges: 1½ Vegetable, 1½ Fat

Herb and Pepper Lentil Stew ♥

Vegetarians all over the world savor lentils for good reason. Not only are lentils hearty and flavorful, they cook up much quicker than dried beans.

Start to finish: 40 minutes **Makes:** 4 servings

1 tablespoon cooking oil
2 medium onions, quartered
1 medium green sweet
    pepper, cut into ½-inch
    rings
1 tablespoon snipped fresh
    thyme or 1 teaspoon
    dried thyme, crushed
¼ teaspoon crushed red
    pepper
3½ cups Vegetable Stock
    (recipe, page 18) or
    two 14½-ounce cans
    vegetable broth
1½ cups water
1¼ cups dry red (Egyptian)
    lentils,* rinsed and
    drained
½ teaspoon salt
    Fresh thyme sprigs

1 In a 4-quart Dutch oven heat oil over medium-high heat. Add onions; cook about 8 minutes or until onions are brown, stirring occasionally.

2 Add green pepper, thyme, and crushed red pepper. Cook and stir for 2 minutes. Add Vegetable Stock, water, 1 cup of the lentils, and salt. Bring to boiling; reduce heat. Simmer, uncovered, for 15 minutes.

3 Stir in remaining lentils. Simmer, uncovered, for 3 to 5 minutes more or until lentils are tender. Season to taste with salt. Garnish with additional fresh thyme.

Nutrition Facts per serving: 256 cal., 5 g total fat (1 g sat. fat), 0 mg chol., 612 mg sodium, 39 g carbo., 10 g fiber, 15 g pro.
Daily Values: 4% vit. A, 41% vit. C, 6% calcium, 18% iron
Exchanges: 2½ Starch, 1 Very Lean Meat, ½ Fat

*Note: You may substitute brown or green lentils for the red lentils. Prepare as directed, except add all of the lentils with water and salt. Bring to boiling; reduce heat. Simmer, covered, for 25 minutes. Simmer, uncovered, about 5 minutes more or until lentils are tender.

Carrot and Chile Pepper Soup ♥ FAST

Sweet baby carrots take on a whole new identity when turned into a special soup revved up with chile peppers and a hint of cumin.

Start to finish: 30 minutes **Makes:** 8 servings

3½ cups Vegetable Stock (recipe, page 18) or two 14½-ounce cans vegetable broth

1 16-ounce package peeled baby carrots

1 large onion, chopped

1 4½-ounce can diced green chile peppers

1 teaspoon chili powder

½ teaspoon ground cumin

1 cup half-and-half or light cream

Salt

1 In a large saucepan or Dutch oven combine the Vegetable Stock, carrots, onion, chile peppers, chili powder, and cumin. Bring to boiling; reduce heat. Simmer, covered, about 12 minutes or until carrots are very tender. Cool slightly.

2 Ladle or pour half of the mixture into a food processor bowl or blender container. Cover and process or blend until smooth. Repeat with the remaining mixture. Return to saucepan. Stir in half-and-half; heat through. Season to taste with salt.

Nutrition Facts per serving: 82 cal., 5 g total fat (2 g sat. fat), 11 mg chol., 227 mg sodium, 8 g carbo., 1 g fiber, 2 g pro.
Daily Values: 5% vit. A, 19% vit. C, 7% calcium, 1% iron
Exchanges: 1½ Vegetable, 1 Fat

Squash Soup with Wheat Berries

Despite a demure demeanor, this golden fruit soup is hot stuff. Giving it bold personality are nuances of Indian curry mixed with hints of garlic, ginger, and red pepper.

Prep: 25 minutes **Cook:** 20 minutes **Makes:** 4 servings

2 cloves garlic, minced
1 tablespoon olive oil
1 teaspoon curry powder
½ teaspoon ground ginger
⅛ teaspoon ground red pepper (optional)
3½ cups Vegetable Stock (recipe, page 18) or two 14½-ounce cans vegetable broth
3 cups chopped, peeled butternut squash
1 cup finely chopped papaya, peaches, or nectarines
Salt
2⅔ cups cooked wheat berries*

1 In a large saucepan cook garlic in hot oil over medium heat for 30 seconds. Add curry powder, ginger, and, if desired, ground red pepper. Cook and stir for 1 minute. Add Vegetable Stock, squash, and papaya. Bring to boiling; reduce heat. Simmer, covered, about 20 minutes or until squash is tender. Cool slightly.

2 Ladle or pour half of the squash mixture into a food processor bowl or blender container. Cover and process or blend until smooth. Repeat with the remaining squash mixture. Return to saucepan; heat through. Season to taste with salt. To serve, divide the wheat berries among 4 soup bowls. Ladle the soup into bowls.

Nutrition Facts per serving: 250 cal., 6 g total fat (1 g sat. fat), 0 mg chol., 310 mg sodium, 48 g carbo., 8 g fiber, 6 g pro.
Daily Values: 166% vit. A, 74% vit. C, 9% calcium, 13% iron
Exchanges: 3 Starch, ½ Fat

*Note: To cook wheat berries, bring 3 cups water to boiling. Stir in 1 cup wheat berries. Return to boiling; reduce heat. Simmer, covered, about 1 hour or until tender; drain. To store, cover and refrigerate up to 3 days. Reheat before serving.

Borscht ♥

Traditionally the beets in this ruby red soup are grated; here, the pieces are cut larger for a chunky version. Note: Beets vary in their sugar content, so you may want to adjust the sugar to taste.

Prep: 20 minutes **Cook:** 30 minutes **Makes:** 4 servings

1½ pounds beets, tops removed
3½ cups Vegetable Stock (recipe, page 18) or two 14½-ounce cans vegetable broth
1½ cups water
2 small onions, halved lengthwise
½ teaspoon salt
2 tablespoons sugar
2 tablespoons lemon juice
¾ cup finely shredded green cabbage

1 Scrub beets; cut off all but 1 inch of stems and roots. Do not peel beets.

2 In a 4-quart Dutch oven combine beets, Vegetable Stock, water, onions, and salt. Bring to boiling; reduce heat. Simmer, covered, for 20 minutes. Using a slotted spoon, remove beets; cool slightly. Slip skins off beets; discard. Cut beets into large pieces. Return to Dutch oven.

3 Stir in sugar and lemon juice. Bring to boiling; reduce heat. Simmer, uncovered, for 10 minutes. Season to taste with salt. If desired, cover and refrigerate.

4 To serve, ladle the soup into bowls, placing an onion half in each bowl. Sprinkle with cabbage.

Nutrition Facts per serving: 127 cal., 2 g total fat (0 g sat. fat), 0 mg chol., 721 mg sodium, 26 g carbo., 5 g fiber, 3 g pro.
Daily Values: 2% vit. A, 25% vit. C, 5% calcium, 8% iron
Exchanges: 3 Vegetable, ½ Other Carbohydrate, ½ Fat

Cheesy Vegetable Chowder

For a crunchy serve-along, make herb bruschetta. Toast a few slices of thick country-style bread under the broiler, rub with a cut garlic clove, drizzle with olive oil, and sprinkle with fresh herbs.

Start to finish: 40 minutes **Makes:** 5 servings

2 cups Vegetable Stock (recipe, page 18) or canned vegetable broth

3 medium potatoes, cubed

¾ cup chopped onion

½ cup chopped celery

1 tablespoon snipped fresh thyme or ½ teaspoon dried thyme, crushed

⅛ teaspoon black pepper

2 cups cut fresh corn or frozen whole kernel corn

2 cups chopped cabbage

¼ cup chopped green sweet pepper

2 cups fat-free milk

2 tablespoons all-purpose flour

1 cup shredded Gruyère or Swiss cheese (4 ounces)

1 In a large saucepan combine the Vegetable Stock, potatoes, onion, celery, thyme, and black pepper. Bring to boiling; reduce heat. Simmer, covered, for 10 minutes. Stir in the corn, cabbage, and green pepper. Simmer, covered, about 5 minutes more or just until potatoes and corn are tender, stirring occasionally.

2 Meanwhile, in a screw-top jar combine ½ cup of the milk and the flour; cover and shake well. Gradually stir the flour mixture into potato mixture. Add the remaining milk.

3 Cook and stir until thickened and bubbly. Cook and stir for 1 minute more. Remove from heat. Stir in cheese until melted.

Nutrition Facts per serving: 304 cal., 9 g total fat (5 g sat. fat), 26 mg chol., 442 mg sodium, 43 g carbo., 5 g fiber, 16 g pro.
Daily Values: 15% vit. A, 71% vit. C, 39% calcium, 10% iron
Exchanges: ½ Milk, 1 Vegetable, 2 Starch, 1 Medium-Fat Meat

Main-Dish Salads

Mexican Fiesta Salad

In this Chapter:

♥ Low-fat and no-fat recipes
* Fast recipes

Fontina and Melon Salad ♥ FAST

Put the "lazy" back in Sundays. Organize brunch around a new take on the fruit-and-cheese course, made quickly with bottled dressing. Accompany with mimosas, the Sunday paper, and a comfy chair.

Start to finish: 25 minutes **Makes:** 4 servings

1½ cups dried large bow tie pasta (about 6 ounces)

⅓ cup bottled fat-free poppy seed salad dressing

1 to 2 tablespoons snipped fresh mint

2 cups cantaloupe and/or honeydew melon chunks

1 cup cubed fontina or Swiss cheese (4 ounces)

2 cups watercress, stems removed

1 Cook pasta according to package directions; drain. Rinse with cold water; drain again.

2 Meanwhile, for dressing, in a small bowl stir together the salad dressing and mint. Set aside.

3 In a large bowl toss together the pasta, cantaloupe and/or honeydew melon, and cheese. Pour the dressing over pasta mixture; toss gently to coat. Serve immediately or cover and refrigerate up to 24 hours.

4 To serve, stir watercress into pasta mixture. If desired, serve salad in melon shells.

Nutrition Facts per serving: 319 cal., 11 g total fat (6 g sat. fat), 73 mg chol., 309 mg sodium, 41 g carbo., 1 g fiber, 14 g pro.
Daily Values: 44% vit. A, 105% vit. C, 18% calcium, 15% iron
Exchanges: ½ Vegetable, ½ Fruit, 2 Starch, 1 Medium-Fat Meat, ½ Fat

Roasted Vegetables over Greens

Grilled Chicken Caesar Salad popularized the idea of serving hot foods over cold greens. You'll love the way the colorful warm veggies make the salad greens wilt pleasantly as they meld.

Prep: 20 minutes **Roast:** 40 minutes **Makes:** 6 servings

12 ounces baby beets or
    3 medium beets
12 ounces tiny new potatoes,
    halved
 4 ounces pearl onions,
    peeled
¼ cup olive oil
 6 cloves garlic, minced
 1 tablespoon snipped fresh
    rosemary or basil or
    1 teaspoon dried
    rosemary or basil,
    crushed
½ teaspoon salt
½ teaspoon coarsely ground
    black pepper
 2 tablespoons balsamic
    vinegar
 1 tablespoon snipped fresh
    chives
 1 tablespoon water
 6 cups torn Boston or Bibb
    lettuce

1 Scrub beets; cut off root and stem ends. (If using medium beets, peel and cut into 1-inch pieces.) In a 13×9×2-inch baking pan combine the beets, potatoes, and onions.

2 In a small bowl combine 2 tablespoons of the oil, the garlic, rosemary, salt, and black pepper. Drizzle over vegetables; toss gently to coat. Cover with foil. Roast in a 375° oven for 30 minutes. Roast, uncovered, for 10 to 20 minutes more or until vegetables are tender. Cool vegetables to room temperature. Drain, reserving pan drippings.

3 For dressing, in a screw-top jar combine the reserved pan drippings, the remaining 2 tablespoons oil, the balsamic vinegar, chives, and water. Cover and shake well. Set aside.

4 Divide the lettuce among 6 dinner plates. Arrange the roasted vegetables on top of lettuce. Shake dressing. Drizzle the dressing over salads.

Nutrition Facts per serving: 172 cal., 9 g total fat (1 g sat. fat), 0 mg chol., 245 mg sodium, 20 g carbo., 3 g fiber, 3 g pro.
Daily Values: 6% vit. A, 30% vit. C, 4% calcium, 7% iron
Exchanges: 2 Vegetable, ½ Starch, 2 Fat

Confetti Barley Salad ♥

No longer sidelined in soups and stews, hearty barley gets center-of-the-plate status in this refreshing, color-studded recipe.

Prep: 15 minutes **Cook:** 45 minutes **Makes:** 6 servings

5 cups water
1 cup pearl barley
2 cups frozen succotash,*
    thawed
¼ cup white wine vinegar
3 tablespoons olive oil
1 tablespoon Dijon-style
    mustard
2 teaspoons snipped fresh
    oregano or ½ teaspoon
    dried oregano, crushed
2 cloves garlic, minced
½ teaspoon salt
¼ teaspoon black pepper
1 cup chopped red sweet
    pepper
½ cup sliced pitted ripe
    olives

1 In a large saucepan bring water to boiling. Stir in barley; reduce heat. Simmer, covered, for 45 to 50 minutes or just until barley is tender, adding succotash the last 10 minutes of cooking; drain. Rinse with cold water; drain again.

2 Meanwhile, for dressing, in a screw-top jar combine the vinegar, oil, mustard, oregano, garlic, salt, and black pepper. Cover and shake well. Set aside.

3 In a large bowl stir together the barley mixture, sweet pepper, and olives. Shake dressing. Pour the dressing over barley mixture; toss gently to coat. Serve immediately or cover and refrigerate up to 24 hours.

Nutrition Facts per serving: 249 cal., 9 g total fat (1 g sat. fat), 0 mg chol., 335 mg sodium, 38 g carbo., 8 g fiber, 6 g pro.
Daily Values: 30% vit. A, 73% vit. C, 4% calcium, 11% iron
Exchanges: 2½ Starch, 1½ Fat

*Note: If you can't find frozen succotash, substitute 1 cup thawed, frozen corn and 1 cup thawed, frozen lima beans.

hearty barley

You're missing out if you haven't tried barley. Its toothsome texture and nutty flavor make it a great choice for pilaf, barley "risotto," salads (see recipe, above) or for adding to soups and casseroles. Look for barley in these forms:

Pearl barley has the outer hull removed and has been polished or "pearled." It is sold in regular or quick-cooking forms.

Scotch or pot barley is less processed than pearl barley. It requires a long soaking period before cooking. Look for it in health food stores.

Barley flakes are similar to rolled oats, but thicker and chewier. Use in homemade granola and in baked goods.

To heighten barley's nutty flavor, take an extra, easy step—toast it before cooking. In a heavy, dry pan over low heat, cook barley about 10 minutes, stirring often, until golden brown.

Nutty Lentil and Brown Rice Salad

Brown rice and lentils bring fullness and satisfaction to this salad. For a gourmet touch, try tiny French green lentils (also called Puy lentils), loved by cooks for their nutty flavor and firm beaded texture.

Prep: 20 minutes **Cook:** 20 minutes **Makes:** 4 servings

4 cups water
1 cup dry lentils, rinsed and drained
½ cup uncooked instant brown rice
⅓ cup white wine vinegar
3 tablespoons olive oil
1 tablespoon snipped fresh thyme or 1 teaspoon dried thyme, crushed
1½ teaspoons sugar
¼ teaspoon salt
⅛ teaspoon black pepper
1 cup coarsely shredded carrots
½ cup chopped red sweet pepper
½ cup chopped pecans, toasted
⅓ cup sliced green onions
Lettuce leaves

1 In a large saucepan combine water and lentils. Bring to boiling; reduce heat. Simmer, covered, for 10 minutes. Stir in rice. Simmer, covered, about 10 minutes more or just until lentils and rice are tender; drain. Rinse with cold water; drain again.

2 Meanwhile, for dressing, in a screw-top jar combine the vinegar, oil, thyme, sugar, salt, and black pepper. Cover and shake well. Set aside.

3 In a large bowl combine the drained lentil mixture, carrots, sweet pepper, pecans, and green onions. Shake dressing. Pour the dressing over lentil mixture; toss gently to coat. Line 4 dinner plates with lettuce leaves; top with salad mixture.

Nutrition Facts per serving: 408 cal., 21 g total fat (2 g sat. fat), 0 mg chol., 164 mg sodium, 42 g carbo., 18 g fiber, 16 g pro.
Daily Values: 178% vit. A, 71% vit. C, 5% calcium, 25% iron
Exchanges: 1 Vegetable, 2½ Starch, 1 Lean Meat, 3 Fat

Note: To make ahead, prepare as directed, except do not add pecans. Cover and refrigerate up to 24 hours. Before serving, stir in pecans.

Italian Bread Salad FAST

Peasant fare—day-old bread, tomatoes, and onions—is a substantial supper fit for any table with well-chosen additions of cheese, basil, and vinaigrette.

Start to finish: 25 minutes **Makes:** 4 servings

5   cups torn bite-size pieces (or 1-inch cubes) day-old Italian or wheat bread
2   cups chopped tomatoes
1   cup cubed fresh mozzarella cheese (4 ounces)
¼   cup finely shredded fresh basil
¼   cup thinly sliced green onions
1   recipe Red Wine Vinaigrette or ½ cup bottled red wine vinaigrette salad dressing

1 In a large bowl toss together the bread, tomatoes, mozzarella cheese, basil, and green onions. Shake Red Wine Vinaigrette. Pour the dressing over bread mixture; toss gently to coat.

Red Wine Vinaigrette: In a screw-top jar combine ¼ cup olive oil; 2 tablespoons red wine vinegar or raspberry vinegar; 1 or 2 cloves garlic, minced; ¼ teaspoon salt; and ¼ teaspoon black pepper. Cover and shake well.

Nutrition Facts per serving: 383 cal., 22 g total fat (6 g sat. fat), 22 mg chol., 582 mg sodium, 35 g carbo., 1 g fiber, 12 g pro.
Daily Values: 14% vit. A, 37% vit. C, 17% calcium, 15% iron
Exchanges: ½ Vegetable, 2 Starch, 1 Medium-Fat Meat, 3 Fat

Deli-Style Pasta Salad ♥ FAST

Thanks to rich, cheese-filled tortellini, a sprinkling of veggies, and a zesty mustard-herb vinaigrette, this pasta salad is in a league of its own.

Start to finish: 25 minutes **Makes:** 4 servings

½ of a 16-ounce package (about 2 cups) frozen cheese-filled tortellini or one 9-ounce package refrigerated cheese-filled tortellini
1½ cups broccoli flowerets
1 large carrot, thinly sliced
¼ cup white wine vinegar
2 tablespoons olive oil
1 teaspoon dried Italian seasoning, crushed
1 teaspoon Dijon-style mustard
¼ teaspoon black pepper
⅛ teaspoon garlic powder
1 medium red or yellow sweet pepper, cut into thin strips
Chive blossoms (optional)

1 In a large saucepan cook pasta according to package directions, except omit any salt and oil. Add broccoli and carrot the last 3 minutes of cooking; drain. Rinse with cold water; drain again.

2 Meanwhile, for dressing, in a screw-top jar combine the vinegar, oil, Italian seasoning, mustard, black pepper, and garlic powder. Cover and shake well. Set aside.

3 In a large bowl combine the pasta mixture and sweet pepper. Shake dressing. Pour the dressing over pasta mixture; toss gently to coat. If desired, garnish with chive blossoms.

Nutrition Facts per serving: 305 cal., 12 g total fat (2 g sat. fat), 30 mg chol., 315 mg sodium, 41 g carbo., 4 g fiber, 13 g pro.
Daily Values: 145% vit. A, 142% vit. C, 14% calcium, 17% iron
Exchanges: 1 Vegetable, 2 Starch, 1 Lean Meat, 1½ Fat

Mexican Fiesta Salad ♥ FAST

Prepare this creamy chilled salad in the morning and look forward all day to a hearty corn-and-bean-studded treat. Lime and cilantro infuse the sour cream dressing.

Start to finish: 30 minutes **Makes:** 4 servings

2 cups dried penne or rotini pasta

½ cup frozen whole kernel corn

½ cup light dairy sour cream

⅓ cup mild or medium chunky salsa

1 tablespoon snipped fresh cilantro

1 tablespoon lime juice

1 15-ounce can black beans, rinsed and drained

3 medium plum tomatoes, chopped (1 cup)

1 medium zucchini, coarsely chopped (1 cup)

½ cup shredded sharp cheddar cheese (2 ounces) (reserve some of the cheese for garnish)

Fresh cilantro (optional)

1 Cook pasta according to package directions, adding corn the last 5 minutes of cooking; drain. Rinse with cold water; drain again.

2 Meanwhile, for dressing, in a small bowl stir together the sour cream, salsa, cilantro, and lime juice. Set aside.

3 In a large bowl combine the pasta mixture, black beans, tomatoes, zucchini, and cheddar cheese. Pour the dressing over pasta mixture; toss gently to coat.

4 Serve immediately or cover and refrigerate up to 24 hours. (After chilling, if desired, stir additional milk into salad to thin dressing to desired consistency.) Top with reserved cheese. If desired, garnish the salad with fresh cilantro.

Nutrition Facts per serving: 373 cal., 9 g total fat (4 g sat. fat), 19 mg chol., 470 mg sodium, 61 g carbo., 7 g fiber, 20 g pro.
Daily Values: 15% vit. A, 36% vit. C, 15% calcium, 23% iron
Exchanges: ½ Vegetable, 4 Starch, 1 Medium-Fat Meat

Tarragon Bean Salad ♥ FAST

This bean-packed salad is loaded with soluble fiber. And with its zippy dressing and vibrant veggies, it's a whole lot more fun to eat than a bowl of oat bran!

Start to finish: 20 minutes **Makes:** 5 servings

1 15-ounce can red kidney beans, rinsed and drained
1 15-ounce can butter beans, rinsed and drained
1 15-ounce can garbanzo beans, rinsed and drained
1½ cups chopped, seeded tomatoes or halved cherry or grape tomatoes
1 medium carrot, cut into thin bite-size strips
2 tablespoons finely chopped red onion
3 tablespoons olive oil
2 tablespoons red wine vinegar
2 tablespoons Dijon-style mustard
1 tablespoon snipped fresh tarragon or ½ teaspoon dried tarragon, crushed
1 teaspoon sugar
¼ teaspoon salt
⅛ teaspoon black pepper
   Boston lettuce leaves

1 In a large bowl combine the beans, tomatoes, carrot, and red onion. For dressing, in a screw-top jar combine the oil, vinegar, mustard, tarragon, sugar, salt, and black pepper. Cover and shake well.

2 Pour the dressing over bean mixture; toss gently to coat. Serve the salad on lettuce-lined dinner plates.

Nutrition Facts per serving: 334 cal., 10 g total fat (1 g sat. fat), 0 mg chol., 1,005 mg sodium, 49 g carbo., 13 g fiber, 14 g pro.
Daily Values: 75% vit. A, 26% vit. C, 9% calcium, 21% iron
Exchanges: 1 Vegetable, 3 Starch, 1½ Fat

Lentil, Corn, and Jicama Salad ♥

Corn lends color and crunch, but the real surprise here is jicama, which lends its clean, crisp bite and mildly sweet flavor to the salad. Look for jicamas that are firm and heavy with unblemished skins.

Prep: 40 minutes **Chill:** 4 hours **Makes:** 4 servings

2½ cups water
1 cup dry lentils
¼ cup chopped onion
¼ teaspoon salt
1 cup frozen whole kernel corn
¾ cup coarsely chopped peeled jicama
½ cup light dairy sour cream
½ cup fat-free mayonnaise dressing or salad dressing
2 tablespoons snipped fresh basil or 1 teaspoon dried basil, crushed
2 tablespoons fat-free milk (optional)
1 medium tomato, seeded and chopped

1 In a medium saucepan combine the water, lentils, onion, and salt. Bring to boiling; reduce heat. Simmer, covered, about 20 minutes or until lentils are tender; drain. In a large bowl combine the lentil mixture and frozen corn; let stand for 10 minutes.

2 Meanwhile, in a medium bowl stir together the jicama, sour cream, mayonnaise dressing, and basil. Pour the sour cream mixture over lentil mixture; toss gently to coat. Cover and refrigerate for 4 to 24 hours, stirring once or twice.

3 To serve, if necessary, stir in enough of the additional milk to thin dressing to desired consistency. Stir in tomato.

Nutrition Facts per serving: 278 cal., 3 g total fat (2 g sat. fat), 10 mg chol., 420 mg sodium, 47 g carbo., 16 g fiber, 17 g pro.
Daily Values: 11% vit. A, 28% vit. C, 9% calcium, 27% iron
Exchanges: 1 Vegetable, 2½ Starch, 1 Lean Meat

love those lentils

Whether lentils really bring wealth and prosperity, as folklore suggests, is open for debate, but one thing is for sure: Lentils are an excellent source of protein. They also supply fiber, calcium, vitamin B, iron, and phosphorus to your diet. With a beanlike texture and a mild, nutty flavor, they're a tasty addition to soups as well as salads, casseroles, and stews.

Grains & Beans

Risotto-Style Barley

In this Chapter:

♥ Low-fat and no-fat recipes
* Fast recipes

Spicy Bulgur-Stuffed Peppers ♥ FAST

This easy stove-top supper—full of Middle Eastern flavors—can appear on your table in half the time of most stuffed-pepper entrées, so it's a good choice on even the busiest of days.

Start to finish: 30 minutes **Makes:** 4 servings

1¾ cups Vegetable Stock (recipe, page 18) or one 14½-ounce can vegetable broth
½ cup shredded carrot
¼ cup chopped onion
3 inches stick cinnamon or dash ground cinnamon
⅛ teaspoon salt
¾ cup bulgur
⅓ cup dried cranberries or raisins
2 large or 4 small sweet peppers, any color*
¾ cup shredded Muenster, brick, or mozzarella cheese (3 ounces)
½ cup water
2 tablespoons sliced almonds or chopped pecans, toasted

1 In a large skillet combine the Vegetable Stock, carrot, onion, cinnamon, and salt. Bring to boiling; reduce heat. Simmer, covered, for 5 minutes. Stir in bulgur and cranberries. Remove from heat. Cover and let stand for 5 minutes; drain. If using stick cinnamon, remove from bulgur mixture.

2 Meanwhile, halve the sweet peppers lengthwise, removing seeds and membranes. Stir the cheese into bulgur mixture. Spoon into sweet pepper halves.

3 Place the sweet pepper halves in skillet, stuffed side up; add water. Bring to boiling; reduce heat. Simmer, covered, for 5 to 10 minutes or until sweet peppers are crisp-tender and bulgur mixture is heated through. Sprinkle with nuts.

Nutrition Facts per serving: 259 cal., 10 g total fat (4 g sat. fat), 20 mg chol., 367 mg sodium, 36 g carbo., 8 g fiber, 10 g pro.
Daily Values: 83% vit. A, 92% vit. C, 19% calcium, 8% iron
Exchanges: 1 Vegetable, 1 Fruit, 1 Starch, 1 Medium-Fat Meat, ½ Fat

*Note: You may substitute 4 large poblano peppers for the sweet peppers. Prepare as directed.

Beans with Spaghetti Squash ♥ FAST

It's not magic, just Mother Nature. When cooked, the golden flesh of spaghetti squash separates into strands that look like the ever-popular pasta. Top the squash with this sassy sauce of sweet-tart beans.

Start to finish: 30 minutes **Makes:** 4 servings

1   2½- to 3-pound spaghetti squash, halved and seeded
1   10-ounce package frozen baby lima beans
1   15-ounce can red kidney beans, rinsed and drained
½   of a 7-ounce jar (½ cup) roasted red sweet peppers, rinsed, drained, and cut into bite-size strips
½   teaspoon salt
¼   cup balsamic vinegar
3   tablespoons olive oil
1   tablespoon honey mustard
2   cloves garlic, minced

1 Place squash halves in a large Dutch oven with about 1 inch of water. Bring to boiling; reduce heat. Cook, covered, for 15 to 20 minutes or until tender.

2 Meanwhile, in a large saucepan cook lima beans according to package directions, adding kidney beans the last 3 minutes of cooking; drain. Return beans to saucepan. Stir in roasted red peppers and salt; heat through.

3 For dressing, in a screw-top jar combine the vinegar, oil, honey mustard, and garlic. Cover and shake well. Pour over warm bean mixture; toss gently to coat.

4 Using a fork, scrape the squash pulp from shells in strands; return strands to each shell. Spoon the warm bean mixture over squash strands in shells; drizzle with any excess dressing. If desired, sprinkle with freshly ground black pepper. To serve, cut each squash shell in half.

Nutrition Facts per serving: 421 cal., 11 g total fat (2 g sat. fat), 0 mg chol., 466 mg sodium, 65 g carbo., 13 g fiber, 21 g pro.
Daily Values: 9% vit. A, 94% vit. C, 6% calcium, 42% iron
Exchanges: 1 Vegetable, 4 Starch, 1 Lean Meat, 1 Fat

Broccoli Rabe over Polenta ♥ FAST

Italians adore chubby broccoli's more slender cruciferous cousin, broccoli rabe (also called rapini). Here, its pleasantly bitter flavor and crunchy texture contrast with the more subtle and creamy polenta.

Start to finish: 30 minutes **Makes:** 4 servings

1   cup quick-cooking polenta
      mix
1   cup Vegetable Stock
      (recipe, page 18) or
      canned vegetable broth
1   tablespoon cornstarch
1   cup chopped sweet onion
      (such as Vidalia or
      Walla Walla)
4   teaspoons olive oil
3   cloves garlic, minced
1   pound broccoli rabe,
      coarsely chopped (about
      7 cups), or 3 cups
      coarsely chopped
      broccoli florets
½   of a 7-ounce jar (½ cup)
      roasted red sweet
      peppers, rinsed,
      drained, and chopped
¼   cup pine nuts or slivered
      almonds, toasted

1 Prepare polenta mix according to package directions. Cover and keep warm. In a small bowl stir together the Vegetable Stock and cornstarch; set aside.

2 In a large skillet cook onion in hot oil over medium heat for 4 to 5 minutes or until tender. Add garlic; cook and stir for 30 seconds. Add broccoli rabe. Cook, covered, about 3 minutes or just until broccoli rabe is tender. (If using broccoli florets, cook and stir for 3 to 4 minutes or until crisp-tender.) Stir in roasted sweet peppers.a

3 Stir the cornstarch mixture; add to vegetable mixture. Cook and stir until thickened and bubbly. Cook and stir for 2 minutes more.

4 To serve, divide the polenta among 4 dinner plates. Spoon the vegetable mixture over polenta. Sprinkle with nuts.

Nutrition Facts per serving: 408 cal., 11 g total fat (2 g sat. fat), 0 mg chol., 118 mg sodium, 69 g carbo., 12 g fiber, 13 g pro.
Daily Values: 33% vit. A, 240% vit. C, 8% calcium, 17% iron
Exchanges: 4 Vegetable, 3 Starch, 1½ Fat

Risotto-Style Barley ♥ FAST

No doubt about it—a vegetable risotto is a great vegetarian main-dish mainstay; here, the concept takes an unexpected turn, with a delightfully nutty barley base.

Start to finish: 30 minutes **Makes:** 4 servings

⅔ cup thinly sliced zucchini
⅓ cup chopped onion
⅓ cup chopped carrot
¼ teaspoon dried rosemary, crushed
⅛ teaspoon black pepper
1 tablespoon olive oil or cooking oil
⅔ cup quick-cooking barley
1¾ cups Vegetable Stock (recipe, page 18) or one 14½-ounce can vegetable broth
¼ cup evaporated milk, half-and-half, or light cream
Salt and black pepper

1 In a medium saucepan cook and stir the zucchini, onion, carrot, rosemary, and black pepper in hot oil just until vegetables are tender. Stir in barley.

2 Meanwhile, in a small saucepan bring Vegetable Stock to boiling. Reduce heat and simmer. Slowly add 1 cup of the stock to barley mixture, stirring constantly. Continue to cook and stir over medium heat until liquid is absorbed. Add the remaining stock, about ¼ cup at a time, stirring constantly until liquid is absorbed. (This should take 10 to 15 minutes total.)

3 Stir in the evaporated milk. Cook and stir for 2 minutes more. Season to taste with salt and additional black pepper.

Nutrition Facts per serving: 155 cal., 6 g total fat (1 g sat. fat), 5 mg chol., 244 mg sodium, 23 g carbo., 3 g fiber, 4 g pro.
Daily Values: 53% vit. A, 5% vit. C, 6% calcium, 4% iron
Exchanges: 1½ Vegetable, 1 Starch, 1 Fat

Mixed Bean Cassoulet ♥

With more kinds of beans in the pot and many of the traditional touches, this meatless rendition achieves the hearty, rustic appeal of a classic French cassoulet.

Prep: 45 minutes **Bake:** 15 minutes **Cook:** 1½ hours **Stand:** 1 hour **Makes:** 6 servings

¾ cup dry Great Northern beans
¾ cup dry pinto beans
½ cup dry garbanzo beans
½ cup chopped celery
½ cup chopped onion
½ cup chopped carrot
1 tablespoon olive oil
3½ cups Vegetable Stock (recipe, page 18) or two 14½-ounce cans vegetable broth
¼ cup water
⅔ cup dried porcini mushrooms
¼ cup bottled roasted red sweet peppers, chopped
¼ cup oil-packed dried tomatoes, drained and snipped
2 tablespoons roasted garlic puree
1 bay leaf
¼ teaspoon salt*
¼ teaspoon dried thyme, crushed
¼ teaspoon dried oregano, crushed
¼ teaspoon black pepper
2 cups soft sourdough bread crumbs
2 tablespoons margarine or butter, melted
1 clove garlic, minced

1 Rinse beans. In a 4-quart Dutch oven combine beans and 8 cups water. Bring to boiling; reduce heat. Simmer, uncovered, for 2 minutes. Remove from heat. Cover and let stand for 1 hour. (Or, place beans in water in Dutch oven. Cover and let soak in a cool place for 6 to 8 hours or overnight.) Drain and rinse beans; set aside.

2 In the same Dutch oven cook the celery, onion, and carrot in hot oil over medium heat about 5 minutes or just until vegetables are tender. Add the drained beans, Vegetable Stock, the ¼ cup water, and dried mushrooms. Bring to boiling; reduce heat. Simmer, covered, for 1 hour.

3 Stir in the roasted red peppers, dried tomatoes, garlic puree, bay leaf, salt, thyme, oregano, and black pepper. Return to boiling; reduce heat. Simmer, covered, about 30 minutes more or until beans are tender and most of the liquid is absorbed. Discard bay leaf.

4 Transfer bean mixture to a 2-quart casserole. In a small bowl combine the bread crumbs, melted margarine, and garlic. Sprinkle over bean mixture. Bake, uncovered, in a 350° oven for 15 to 20 minutes or until bread crumbs are lightly toasted.

Nutrition Facts per serving: 358 cal., 11 g total fat (2 g sat. fat), 0 mg chol., 435 mg sodium, 52 g carbo., 15 g fiber, 15 g pro.
Daily Values: 57% vit. A, 45% vit. C, 11% calcium, 21% iron
Exchanges: 1 Vegetable, 3 Starch, 1 Very Lean Meat, 1½ Fat

*Note: If using canned vegetable broth, omit the salt.

Savory Beans and Rice ♥

For a mild flavor, use only a drop or two of hot pepper sauce. If you like lots of heat, dash in a little more.

Prep: 20 minutes **Cook:** 1 hour 40 minutes **Stand:** 1 hour **Makes:** 5 servings

1¼ cups dry red beans or dry red kidney beans
2½ cups Vegetable Stock (recipe, page 18) or canned vegetable broth
¾ cup chopped onion
½ cup sliced celery
1 teaspoon dried basil, crushed
2 cloves garlic, minced
1 bay leaf
1¼ cups uncooked regular brown rice
1 14½-ounce can low-sodium stewed tomatoes, undrained
1 4½-ounce can diced green chile peppers, drained
Few dashes bottled hot pepper sauce

1 Rinse beans. In a large saucepan combine beans and 4 cups water. Bring to boiling; reduce heat. Simmer, uncovered, for 2 minutes. Remove from heat. Cover and let stand for 1 hour. (Or, place beans in water in saucepan. Cover and let soak in a cool place for 6 to 8 hours or overnight.) Drain and rinse beans.

2 In the same saucepan combine the beans, Vegetable Stock, onion, celery, basil, garlic, and bay leaf. Bring to boiling; reduce heat. Simmer, covered, for 1½ to 1¾ hours or until beans are tender, stirring occasionally. Discard bay leaf.

3 Meanwhile, cook brown rice according to package directions, except omit any salt. Cover and keep warm.

4 Stir the tomatoes, chile peppers, and hot pepper sauce into bean mixture. Bring to boiling; reduce heat. Simmer, uncovered, about 10 minutes more or until desired consistency. Season to taste with salt. Serve the bean mixture over brown rice.

Nutrition Facts per serving: 376 cal., 3 g total fat (0 g sat. fat), 0 mg chol., 282 mg sodium, 73 g carbo., 11 g fiber, 16 g pro.
Daily Values: 1% vit. A, 28% vit. C, 10% calcium, 20% iron
Exchanges: 1 Vegetable, 4½ Starch

Creamy Barley and Broccoli FAST

A little like a creamy risotto, this dish gets its wonderful richness from sweet and nutty Gruyère cheese, which typically hails from Switzerland (French Gruyère works well too).

Start to finish: 25 minutes **Makes:** 4 servings

1¾ cups Vegetable Stock (recipe, page 18) or one 14½-ounce can vegetable broth
1 cup quick-cooking barley
2 cups broccoli florets
2 tablespoons margarine or butter
2 tablespoons all-purpose flour
¼ teaspoon salt
   Dash ground allspice
1½ cups light milk
¾ cup shredded Gruyère cheese (3 ounces)
   Cracked pink peppercorns

1 In a medium saucepan bring Vegetable Stock to boiling. Stir in barley. Return to boiling; reduce heat. Simmer, covered, for 10 to 12 minutes or until barley is tender and most of the liquid is absorbed, adding broccoli the last 5 minutes of cooking.

2 Meanwhile, for sauce, in a small saucepan melt margarine. Stir in flour, salt, and allspice. Add milk all at once. Cook and stir over medium heat until thickened and bubbly. Cook and stir for 1 minute more. Stir in ½ cup of the cheese until melted.

3 Gently stir the sauce into barley mixture. Divide the barley mixture among 4 shallow pasta bowls. Sprinkle with the remaining cheese and pink peppercorns.

Nutrition Facts per serving: 343 cal., 16 g total fat (6 g sat. fat), 30 mg chol., 492 mg sodium, 38 g carbo., 5 g fiber, 15 g pro.
Daily Values: 27% vit. A, 60% vit. C, 36% calcium, 8% iron
Exchanges: 1 Vegetable, 2 Starch, 1 High-Fat Meat, 1 Fat

pepper genealogy

Where do peppercorns come from? Three of the most popular types come from the pepper plant (*Piper nigrum*). Black peppercorns are berries from this plant that are picked before they're ripe and dried until they shrivel and turn dark. White peppercorns are the same berries that are allowed to ripen, then are dried and hulled to expose a white creamy core. Green peppercorns are immature pepper berries that are picked while they're still tender and are usually preserved in brine—although they can be packed in water, dried, or freeze-dried. Pink peppercorns aren't true pepper at all; they're the dried berries of a variety of rose plant. Szechwan peppercorns come from an ash tree and have a tiny seed inside each berry. They have a distinctive flavor and aroma and often are used in Oriental dishes.

Saffron Pilaf & Grilled Vegetables ♥

Similar to paella—Spain's national dish—this sunny-colored saffron rice dish is bursting with flavor from a rainbow of grilled vegetables, instead of the standard shrimp and meat.

Prep: 25 minutes **Grill:** 10 minutes **Makes:** 4 servings

1¾ cups Vegetable Stock (recipe, page 18) or one 14½-ounce can vegetable broth
1 cup uncooked jasmine, basmati, or wild-pecan rice
¼ cup water
⅛ teaspoon thread saffron or dash ground saffron*
2 tablespoons olive oil
½ teaspoon bottled minced garlic
1 eggplant, sliced ½ inch thick
1 large zucchini, halved lengthwise
1 red sweet pepper, quartered
   Salt and black pepper
1 ounce herbed semisoft goat cheese (chèvre), crumbled
2 tablespoons coarsely chopped hazelnuts or pecans, toasted

1 In a large saucepan combine the Vegetable Stock, rice, water, and saffron. Bring to boiling; reduce heat. Simmer, covered, about 15 minutes or until rice is tender and liquid is absorbed. Cover and keep warm.

2 Meanwhile, in a small bowl combine the oil and garlic. Brush over the eggplant, zucchini, and sweet pepper.

3 Grill vegetables on the lightly greased rack of an uncovered grill directly over medium coals about 10 minutes or until vegetables are tender, turning once halfway through grilling. Season to taste with salt and black pepper.

4 Transfer the vegetables to a cutting board; cool slightly. Cut vegetables into bite-size pieces; stir into cooked rice. Transfer the pilaf to a serving dish. Sprinkle with goat cheese and nuts.

Nutrition Facts per serving: 325 cal., 12 g total fat (2 g sat. fat), 3 mg chol., 183 mg sodium, 48 g carbo., 5 g fiber, 7 g pro.
Daily Values: 34% vit. A, 83% vit. C, 5% calcium, 17% iron
Exchanges: 1½ Vegetable, 2½ Starch, 2 Fat

*Note: You may substitute ¼ teaspoon ground turmeric for the saffron.

Southwestern Black Bean Cakes FAST

These spicy bean cakes are flavored with a chipotle—a dried, smoked jalapeño pepper—that comes in adobo sauce, a Mexican melange of ground chile peppers, herbs, and vinegar.

Prep: 20 minutes **Grill:** 8 minutes **Makes:** 4 servings

½ of a medium avocado, seeded and peeled
1 tablespoon lime juice
Salt and black pepper
2 slices whole wheat bread, torn
3 tablespoons fresh cilantro leaves
2 cloves garlic
1 15-ounce can black beans, rinsed and drained
1 canned chipotle pepper in adobo sauce
1 to 2 teaspoons adobo sauce
1 teaspoon ground cumin
1 egg
1 small plum tomato, chopped

1 For guacamole, in a small bowl mash avocado. Stir in lime juice; season to taste with salt and black pepper. Cover surface with plastic wrap and set aside until ready to serve.

2 Place torn bread in a food processor bowl or blender container. Cover and process or blend until bread resembles coarse crumbs; transfer to a large bowl and set aside.

3 Place cilantro and garlic in the food processor bowl or blender container; cover and process or blend until finely chopped. Add the beans, chipotle pepper, adobo sauce, and cumin. Cover and process or blend using on/off pulses until beans are coarsely chopped and mixture begins to pull away from sides. Add mixture to bread crumbs in bowl. Add egg; mix well. Shape into four ½-inch-thick patties.

4 Grill patties on the lightly greased rack of an uncovered grill directly over medium coals for 8 to 10 minutes or until patties are heated through, turning once halfway through grilling. Serve the patties with guacamole and tomato.

Nutrition Facts per serving: 178 cal., 7 g total fat (1 g sat. fat), 53 mg chol., 487 mg sodium, 25 g carbo., 9 g fiber, 11 g pro.
Daily Values: 9% vit. A, 12% vit. C, 7% calcium, 16% iron
Exchanges: 1½ Starch, 1 Lean Meat, ½ Fat

Hoppin' John with Grits Polenta

Southerners claim Hoppin' John brings good luck when eaten on New Year's Day. Vegetarians who want a good, down-home meatless feast will feel lucky any time this recipe comes to the table.

Prep: 50 minutes **Chill:** 2 hours **Makes:** 6 servings

1   recipe Grits Polenta
¾   cup uncooked long grain rice
½   of a 16-ounce package frozen black-eyed peas or one 15-ounce can black-eyed peas, rinsed and drained
1½ cups chopped red, yellow, and/or green sweet peppers
1   cup thinly bias-sliced carrots
1   cup frozen whole kernel corn
1   tablespoon finely chopped shallot or onion
4   cloves garlic, minced
2   teaspoons snipped fresh thyme or 1 teaspoon dried thyme, crushed
¼   teaspoon salt
¼   teaspoon crushed red pepper
⅛   teaspoon black pepper
2   teaspoons olive oil or cooking oil
2   medium tomatoes, seeded and chopped
2   tablespoons snipped fresh parsley

1 Prepare Grits Polenta. Cover and refrigerate at least 2 hours or until firm. Cook rice according to package directions, except omit any salt. If using frozen black-eyed peas, cook peas according to package directions; drain.

2 In a covered 12-inch skillet cook sweet peppers, carrots, corn, shallot, garlic, thyme, salt, crushed red pepper, and black pepper in hot oil for 6 to 8 minutes or until crisp-tender, stirring occasionally. Stir in cooked rice, black-eyed peas, and tomatoes. Cook, covered, over low heat about 5 minutes or until heated through, stirring occasionally. Stir in parsley.

3 Meanwhile, cut the grits mixture into 12 wedges. Arrange on the greased unheated rack of a broiler pan. Broil 4 to 5 inches from the heat for 4 to 5 minutes or until wedges begin to brown. Serve with rice mixture. Garnish with additional fresh thyme.

Grits Polenta: Combine 1⅓ cups water, ⅔ cup fat-free milk, and ⅛ teaspoon salt. Bring to boiling; reduce heat. Slowly add ½ cup quick-cooking white (hominy) grits, stirring with a whisk. Cook and stir for 5 to 7 minutes or until very thick. Remove from heat. Stir in ½ cup shredded reduced-fat mozzarella cheese until melted. Spread in a greased 9-inch pie plate.

Nutrition Facts per serving: 284 cal., 4 g total fat (1 g sat. fat), 5 mg chol., 242 mg sodium, 52 g carbo., 6 g fiber, 12 g pro.
Daily Values: 155% vit. A, 124% vit. C, 15% calcium, 17% iron
Exchanges: 2 Vegetable, 3 Starch

Sweet Onion and Rice Casserole

Comforting casseroles need not be unsophisticated. With fresh mushrooms and specialty onions, this contemporary casserole is better served with a glass of wine than a glass of milk.

Prep: 45 minutes **Bake:** 30 minutes **Makes:** 6 to 8 servings

3 cups water

½ teaspoon salt

1½ cups uncooked Arborio rice or short grain rice

¼ cup margarine or butter

1 cup whole fresh mushrooms (such as porcini and/or button)

12 purple or white boiling onions, peeled and halved

1 medium sweet onion (such as Vidalia or Walla Walla), cut into 8 wedges

2 cloves garlic, minced

1¾ cups Vegetable Stock (recipe, page 18) or one 14½-ounce can vegetable broth

¾ cup freshly shredded Romano or Parmesan cheese

1 In a medium saucepan combine water and salt. Bring to boiling. Remove from heat; stir in rice. Cover and let stand for 30 minutes; drain. Rinse with cold water; drain again.

2 Meanwhile, in a large skillet melt margarine over medium-high heat. Add one-third of the mushrooms; cook and stir for 4 to 5 minutes or until tender. Remove mushrooms.

3 Add the remaining mushrooms, boiling onions, sweet onion, and garlic to hot skillet. Cook and stir until vegetables are tender. Add rice; reduce heat to medium. Cook and stir for 4 to 5 minutes or until rice is golden brown. Carefully stir in Vegetable Stock. Bring to boiling. Transfer to a 2-quart soufflé dish or casserole.

4 Bake, covered, in a 325° oven for 25 to 30 minutes or until rice is tender and liquid is absorbed. Fluff with a fork. Stir in ⅔ cup of the Romano cheese. Sprinkle with the remaining cheese and the reserved cooked mushrooms. Bake, uncovered, about 5 minutes more or until cheese is melted and lightly browned.

Nutrition Facts per serving: 313 cal., 12 g total fat (2 g sat. fat), 8 mg chol., 523 mg sodium, 43 g carbo., 2 g fiber, 8 g pro.
Daily Values: 7% vit. A, 3% vit. C, 11% calcium, 12% iron
Exchanges: 3 Starch, 2 Fat

types of white rice

When cooking white rice for recipes, you can choose from three types: **Short grain rice** is high in starch, making it stickier than other rices. It is most often used in Asian cooking, Spanish paella, and risotto. One prized short grain rice is Arborio rice—a mainstay for risotto. **Medium grain rice** is slightly sticky. It cooks up tender and plump with a mild flavor and can be used in a variety of dishes. **Long grain white rice** is the most common rice used in America. It has a neutral taste and firm texture, and remains separate and fluffy when cooked. Long grain rices such as jasmine and basmati are aromatic rices known for their fragrances. Both are nice paired with stir-fry dishes and other Asian- and Indian-style foods or used in pilafs.

Spinach Risotto and Acorn Squash ♥

Stubby Arborio rice—the key to authentic risottos—creates a luscious dish. During cooking, the grains soften and their special starch transforms the broth into a creamy, unforgettable sauce.

Start to finish: 35 minutes **Makes:** 4 servings

1 1½- to 2-pound acorn or butternut squash, halved lengthwise and seeded
1 cup chopped red onion
4 cloves garlic, minced
1 tablespoon olive oil
1 cup uncooked Arborio rice or short grain rice
3 cups Vegetable Stock (recipe, page 18) or vegetable broth
3 cups packed chopped spinach
2 tablespoons finely shredded Parmesan cheese

1 Cut each squash half crosswise into 1-inch slices. In a covered Dutch oven cook squash in a small amount of boiling water for 10 to 15 minutes or until tender. Drain and keep warm.

2 Meanwhile, in a large saucepan cook onion and garlic in hot oil over medium heat for 4 to 5 minutes or until onion is tender. Add rice; cook and stir for 1 minute more.

3 In a medium saucepan bring Vegetable Stock to boiling. Reduce heat and simmer. Slowly add 1 cup of the stock to rice mixture, stirring constantly. Continue to cook and stir over medium heat until liquid is absorbed. Add another ½ cup of the stock to rice mixture, stirring constantly. Continue to cook and stir until liquid is absorbed. Add another 1 cup stock, ½ cup at a time, stirring constantly until liquid is absorbed. (This should take about 15 minutes total.)

4 Stir in the remaining ½ cup stock. Cook and stir just until rice is tender and slightly creamy. Stir in spinach and Parmesan cheese. Season to taste with salt. Serve the risotto with squash slices.

Nutrition Facts per serving: 321 cal., 7 g total fat (1 g sat. fat), 3 mg chol., 330 mg sodium, 59 g carbo., 7 g fiber, 8 g pro.
Daily Values: 157% vit. A, 44% vit. C, 12% calcium, 27% iron
Exchanges: 1 Vegetable, 3½ Starch, ½ Fat

Poached Eggs with Polenta and Beans

In this Chapter:

♥ Low-fat and no-fat recipes
* Fast recipes

Corn and Tomato Bread Pudding ♥

The proof of a delicious dinner is in this pudding, a classic dessert reinvented as a savory main course. Use only firm, day-old (or older) bread, as fresh bread is too soft to soak up all the milk and eggs.

Prep: 20 minutes **Bake:** 30 minutes **Stand:** 5 minutes **Makes:** 6 servings

3 tablespoons snipped dried tomatoes (not oil-packed)

4 eggs

1½ cups milk, half-and-half, or light cream

1 tablespoon snipped fresh basil or 1 teaspoon dried basil, crushed

4 cups torn English muffins or dry French bread

1½ cups cut fresh corn or frozen whole kernel corn

1 cup shredded reduced-fat cheddar cheese or Monterey Jack cheese with jalapeño peppers (4 ounces)

1 tomato, cut into thin wedges (optional)

1 Place dried tomatoes in a small bowl and cover with hot water. Let stand about 15 minutes or until softened; drain.

2 Meanwhile, in a medium bowl beat together the eggs, milk, and basil; set aside. In an ungreased 2-quart square baking dish toss together the English muffins, corn, cheese, and softened tomatoes.* Carefully pour the egg mixture evenly over English muffin mixture. Gently press down English muffins with the back of a spoon to moisten with egg mixture.

3 Bake, uncovered, in a 375° oven about 30 minutes or until a knife inserted near center comes out clean. Let stand for 5 to 10 minutes before serving. If desired, serve the bread pudding on top of tomato wedges.

Nutrition Facts per serving: 275 cal., 9 g total fat (4 g sat. fat), 160 mg chol., 486 mg sodium, 32 g carbo., 3 g fiber, 16 g pro.
Daily Values: 14% vit. A, 6% vit. C, 23% calcium, 11% iron
Exchanges: ½ Milk, 1½ Starch, 1½ Lean Meat

***Note:** To make ahead, cover and refrigerate the egg mixture and English muffin mixture separately up to 24 hours. Combine and bake as directed.

Curried Eggs with Rice and Lentils

This recipe is based on an East Indian dish called kedgeree (kehj-uh-REE). The addition of a few eggs makes it similar to an English take on the dish.

Start to finish: 35 minutes   **Makes:** 4 to 5 servings

3   tablespoons olive oil
1   cup chopped onion
2   teaspoons curry powder
1   cup uncooked basmati rice
3   cups Vegetable Stock
      (recipe, page 18),
      canned vegetable broth,
      or water
½   cup dry lentils
3   beaten eggs
¼   cup dairy sour cream
½   teaspoon salt
¼   teaspoon ground nutmeg
¼   teaspoon black pepper
¼   cup snipped fresh cilantro
      or Italian flat-leaf
      parsley

1 In a large saucepan heat 2 tablespoons of the oil over medium heat. Add onion and curry powder; cook and stir for 3 to 5 minutes or until onion is almost tender. Add rice; cook and stir for 3 minutes. Add Vegetable Stock and lentils. Bring to boiling; reduce heat. Simmer, covered, for 20 to 25 minutes or just until lentils are tender and liquid is absorbed. (Do not overcook.)

2 Meanwhile, pour the remaining 1 tablespoon oil into a wok or large skillet. Heat wok over medium heat. Pour the eggs into hot wok; lift and tilt the wok until eggs form a thin sheet. Cook, without stirring, about 2 minutes or just until eggs are set. Slide out onto a cutting board. Cut into ¾-inch strips; set aside.

3 In a small bowl combine the sour cream, salt, nutmeg, and black pepper. Stir into the rice mixture. Stir in the egg strips just until combined. To serve, sprinkle each serving with cilantro.

Nutrition Facts per serving: 436 cal., 19 g total fat (4 g sat. fat), 165 mg chol., 607 mg sodium, 52 g carbo., 11 g fiber, 16 g pro.
Daily Values: 13% vit. A, 9% vit. C, 9% calcium, 23% iron
Exchanges: 3½ Starch, 1 Medium-Fat Meat, 2 Fat

types of lentils

Lentils are a favorite food in France, the Middle East, and India where they are used in soups, stews, and other main dishes. There are three common types: the brown lentil, which actually has a greenish-brown coat and a yellow interior; the red lentil; and the yellow lentil. In food specialty stores, more exotic varieties, such as green, white, or black, also are available.

In the United States, the brown lentil is the most common type and is most often used in recipes. If you wish to substitute one type of lentil for another, you may need to adjust the cooking time. If you're using yellow lentils, the cooking time will be the same as for brown lentils. For the red varieties, which are smaller, you'll need to reduce the time significantly. Check package directions for cooking times.

Grecian Quiches

Kalamata olives and feta cheese add quintessential Greek touches to the classic quiche. Serve these mini quiches with fruit salad for brunch, or a mixed greens salad for a lunch or light supper.

Prep: 35 minutes **Bake:** 20 minutes **Stand:** 5 minutes **Makes:** 8 servings

1 recipe Herb Crust
1 tablespoon butter or margarine
2½ cups sliced fresh mushrooms
¼ cup finely chopped shallots
¼ cup chopped pitted kalamata olives
1 4-ounce jar sliced pimientos, drained
2 eggs
½ cup milk
½ teaspoon dry mustard
¼ teaspoon salt
¼ teaspoon black pepper
½ cup crumbled feta cheese (2 ounces) (optional)

1 Prepare Herb Crust. To make individual quiches, divide the dough into 8 portions. On a lightly floured surface, slightly flatten one portion of dough. Roll the dough from center to edges into a 5-inch circle. Place in a 4×1-inch fluted tart pan with a removable bottom. Press dough into fluted sides of pan; trim edges even with sides. Repeat with the remaining dough.

2 Place tart pans in a shallow baking pan. Line each tart pan with a double thickness of foil. Bake in a 450° oven for 8 minutes. Remove foil; bake for 4 to 5 minutes more or until pastry is set and dry. Cool on a wire rack. (Or, to make a single large quiche, do not divide dough. Roll dough into a 12-inch circle. Place in a 9-inch fluted tart pan with a removable bottom. Press dough into fluted sides; trim edges. Line with a double thickness of foil. Bake in a 450° oven for 8 minutes. Remove foil; bake about 10 minutes more. Cool.) Reduce oven temperature to 375°.

3 In a large skillet melt butter over medium-high heat. Add mushrooms; cook and stir for 4 to 5 minutes or until tender. Remove from heat. Stir in shallots, olives, and pimientos. Spoon the mixture evenly into prebaked tart shell(s); set aside.

4 In a small bowl beat together the eggs, milk, dry mustard, salt, and black pepper. Carefully pour over mushroom mixture. Bake in the 375° oven for 20 to 25 minutes or just until set and a knife inserted near center(s) comes out clean. If desired, sprinkle with cheese. Let stand for 5 minutes before serving.

Herb Crust: In a medium bowl stir together 1½ cups all-purpose flour; 2 teaspoons dried herbes de Provence, crushed; and ½ teaspoon salt. Using a pastry blender, cut in ½ cup cold butter until pieces are pea-size. Add 5 to 6 tablespoons cold water, 1 tablespoon at a time, tossing gently until all the dough is moistened. Form dough into a ball.

Nutrition Facts per serving: 247 cal., 17 g total fat (9 g sat. fat), 91 mg chol., 431 mg sodium, 20 g carbo., 1 g fiber, 6 g pro.
Daily Values: 17% vit. A, 9% vit. C, 4% calcium, 9% iron
Exchanges: 1 Vegetable, 1 Starch, 3 Fat

Mediterranean Strata ♥

Mediterranean cooks are masters at stretching meat (or forgoing it entirely) and creating vibrant foods. With its spark of green olives and the sweetness of roasted peppers, this dish provides a fine example.

Prep: 20 minutes **Bake:** 35 minutes **Stand:** 5 minutes **Makes:** 8 servings

3 cups cubed Italian bread
2 large onions, thinly sliced
2 teaspoons bottled minced garlic
2 tablespoons olive oil
½ cup chopped bottled roasted red sweet peppers
½ cup chopped pitted green olives
½ cup crumbled feta cheese (2 ounces)
6 eggs
1¾ cups Vegetable Stock (recipe, page 18) or one 14½-ounce can vegetable broth
¼ cup dry white wine
¼ teaspoon black pepper

1 Arrange the Italian bread cubes in a greased 10-inch quiche dish; set aside.

2 In a large skillet cook onions and garlic in hot oil over medium heat about 10 minutes or until onions are golden brown, stirring frequently. Remove from heat. Stir in the roasted red peppers and olives. Spoon the onion mixture over bread cubes. Sprinkle with the feta cheese.

3 In a large bowl beat together the eggs, Vegetable Stock, wine, and black pepper. Carefully pour evenly over bread mixture. Gently press down bread with the back of a spoon to moisten with egg mixture.

4 Bake, uncovered, in a 350° oven for 35 to 45 minutes or until a knife inserted near center comes out clean. Let stand for 5 to 10 minutes before serving.

Nutrition Facts per serving: 173 cal., 11 g total fat (3 g sat. fat), 166 mg chol., 515 mg sodium, 11 g carbo., 1 g fiber, 8 g pro.
Daily Values: 12% vit. A, 46% vit. C, 6% calcium, 9% iron
Exchanges: ½ Vegetable, ½ Starch, 1 Medium-Fat Meat, 1 Fat

Miniature Mexican Frittatas

These spunky little egg casseroles are baked in muffin cups and served with salsa. They make great breakfast or brunch fare.

Prep: 15 miniutes **Bake:** 20 minutes **Stand:** 5 minutes **Makes:** 4 servings

1 10-ounce package frozen chopped spinach, thawed and well drained
1 cup cottage cheese, drained
½ cup grated Parmesan cheese
½ cup shredded cheddar cheese (2 ounces)
4 eggs
¼ cup milk
1 teaspoon ground cumin
¼ teaspoon black pepper
2 tablespoons snipped fresh cilantro or parsley
½ cup salsa, warmed
  Dairy sour cream (optional)

1 In a medium bowl combine the spinach, cottage cheese, Parmesan cheese, and cheddar cheese. In a small bowl beat together the eggs, milk, cumin, and black pepper. Stir the egg mixture into spinach mixture. Stir in the cilantro.

2 Spoon the egg mixture into 12 lightly greased 2½-inch muffin cups. Bake, uncovered, in a 375° oven for 20 to 25 minutes or until egg mixture is set. Let stand for 5 minutes. Remove from muffin cups. Serve with salsa and, if desired, sour cream.

Nutrition Facts per serving: 278 cal., 16 g total fat (9 g sat. fat), 246 mg chol., 737 mg sodium, 9 g carbo., 3 g fiber, 25 g pro.
Daily Values: 129% vit. A, 20% vit. C, 46% calcium, 13% iron
Exchanges: 2 Vegetable, 3 Medium-Fat Meat

egg substitutes

Refrigerated or frozen egg substitutes are easy to use, readily available, and enable anyone on a cholesterol-restricted diet to enjoy great-tasting egg dishes. These products are based mostly on egg whites, contain less fat than whole eggs, and have no cholesterol. I use ¼ cup of either the refrigerated or thawed frozen egg product for each whole egg in scrambled egg dishes, omelets, quiches, frittatas, and stratas. To replace hard-cooked eggs in salads and other recipes, I cook the egg product as I'd cook an omelet and cut it into bite-size pieces.

Jill Moberly

Test Kitchen Home Economist

Ranch Eggs

Your taste buds will get a wake-up call with this Mexican-style casserole. If hot-and-spicy doesn't suit you in the morning, serve this meatless main dish for supper.

Prep: 10 minutes **Bake:** 21 minutes **Makes:** 6 servings

1 large onion, halved lengthwise and thinly sliced
1 15-ounce can chunky chili-style tomato sauce
3 tablespoons snipped fresh cilantro
1 fresh jalapeño pepper, seeded and chopped
6 eggs
¼ teaspoon salt
⅛ teaspoon black pepper
1 cup shredded Monterey Jack or cheddar cheese (4 ounces)
  Flour tortillas, warmed, or toast

1 Separate the onion into half-rings and place in a greased 2-quart rectangular baking dish.

2 In a small bowl stir together the tomato sauce, cilantro, and jalapeño pepper. Pour the tomato mixture over onion. Break one of the eggs into a measuring cup. Carefully slide egg into tomato mixture. Repeat with the remaining eggs. Sprinkle the eggs with salt and black pepper.

3 Bake, uncovered, in a 400° oven for 20 to 25 minutes or until the egg whites are completely set and yolks begin to thicken but are not hard. Sprinkle with cheese. Bake, uncovered, for 1 minute more. Serve with tortillas.

Nutrition Facts per serving: 270 cal., 13 g total fat (6 g sat. fat), 230 mg chol., 736 mg sodium, 26 g carbo., 0 g fiber, 15 g pro.
Daily Values: 23% vit. A, 19% vit. C, 19% calcium, 16% iron
Exchanges: 1 Vegetable, 1½ Starch, 1½ Medium-Fat Meat

Poached Eggs with Polenta and Beans

This Southwestern-inspired creation offers a great way to take advantage of the easy-to-use tubes of prepared polenta found in the produce aisle.

Start to finish: 35 minutes **Makes:** 4 servings

3 medium plum tomatoes, seeded and chopped
½ cup canned black beans, rinsed and drained
2 tablespoons chopped red onion
1 fresh jalapeño pepper, seeded and finely chopped
1 tablespoon snipped fresh cilantro
2 teaspoons balsamic vinegar
1 teaspoon olive oil
⅛ teaspoon salt
⅛ teaspoon black pepper
1 16-ounce tube refrigerated plain cooked polenta
1 tablespoon olive oil
4 eggs
2 teaspoons snipped fresh cilantro
Fresh cilantro (optional)
Lime wedges

1 For salsa, combine tomatoes, beans, onion, jalapeño pepper, the 1 tablespoon cilantro, the balsamic vinegar, the 1 teaspoon oil, the salt, and black pepper. Set aside until ready to serve. Unwrap the polenta and cut into 12 slices. In a 12-inch nonstick skillet heat the 1 tablespoon oil over medium heat. Add polenta. Cook for 14 to 16 minutes or until browned, turning once.

2 Meanwhile, to poach eggs, fill a large skillet half full with water. Bring to boiling; reduce heat to simmering. Break one of the eggs into a measuring cup. Carefully slide egg into simmering water, holding the lip of cup close to water. Repeat with the remaining eggs. Simmer, uncovered, for 3 to 5 minutes or until the egg whites are completely set and yolks begin to thicken but are not hard. Using a slotted spoon, remove eggs.

3 Serve the polenta with salsa and poached eggs. Season eggs to taste with additional salt and black pepper. Sprinkle with the 2 teaspoons cilantro. If desired, garnish with additional fresh cilantro. Serve with lime wedges.

Nutrition Facts per serving: 254 cal., 10 g total fat (2 g sat. fat), 213 mg chol., 768 mg sodium, 29 g carbo., 6 g fiber, 11 g pro.
Daily Values: 13% vit. A, 16% vit. C, 4% calcium, 9% iron
Exchanges: 1 Vegetable, 1½ Starch, 1 Lean Meat, 1 Fat

Cheese Frittata with Mushrooms FAST

The fuss-free Italian frittata is far easier to make than its French cousin, the omelet. This spur-of-the-moment skillet supper is terrific with a loaf of crusty peasant-style bread.

Start to finish: 25 minutes Makes: 4 servings

6 eggs
⅓ cup shredded Gruyère or Swiss cheese
¼ cup water
¼ teaspoon salt
⅛ teaspoon freshly ground black pepper
2 tablespoons margarine or butter
1½ cups thinly sliced fresh mushrooms (such as shiitake, chanterelle, brown, or button)
¼ cup sliced green onions
1 tablespoon snipped fresh Italian flat-leaf parsley
1 tablespoon snipped fresh dill

1 In a medium bowl beat together the eggs, cheese, water, salt, and black pepper; set aside.

2 In a 10-inch nonstick skillet melt margarine over medium-high heat. Add mushrooms; cook and stir for 4 to 5 minutes or until liquid is evaporated. Stir in green onions, parsley, and dill.

3 Pour the egg mixture into skillet over mushroom mixture. Cook, uncovered, over medium heat. As the egg mixture begins to set, run a spatula around edges of skillet, lifting egg mixture so the uncooked portion flows underneath. Continue cooking and lifting edges until the egg mixture is almost set (surface will be moist). Remove from heat.

4 Cover and let stand for 3 to 4 minutes or until top is set. Cut into wedges.

Nutrition Facts per serving: 216 cal., 17 g total fat (5 g sat. fat), 331 mg chol., 332 mg sodium, 3 g carbo., 0 g fiber, 13 g pro.
Daily Values: 26% vit. A, 5% vit. C, 12% calcium, 11% iron
Exchanges: ½ Vegetable, 2 Medium-Fat Meat, 1½ Fat

easy herbs

In most dishes featuring herbs, fresh is best. Here's how I easily prepare fresh herbs for use in cooking:

Herbs with delicate stems, such as cilantro, parsley, basil, and mint, can simply be snipped—stems and all—in a small bowl with a pair of clean kitchen shears. I find this is often much faster and neater than chopping the herbs on a cutting board.

Herbs with woodier stems, such as thyme, oregano, and particularly rosemary, should be stripped from their stems before using. I hold the stem in one hand, and—starting at the top of the stem—strip off the leaves by running the fingers of my other hand firmly down the stem.

Lori Wilson
Test Kitchen Home Economist

Summertime Eggplant and Herbs

Pasta

In this Chapter:

♥ Low-fat and no-fat recipes
* Fast recipes

Pasta with Red Pepper Sauce ♥

This vibrant red sauce is a versatile standby in a vegetarian cook's repertoire. Experiment using it over polenta, vegetables, and in other dishes for a change of pace from your favorite marinara sauce.

Start to finish: 35 minutes **Makes:** 4 servings

6   medium red sweet peppers, chopped, or two 12-ounce jars roasted red sweet peppers, drained
4   cloves garlic
2   tablespoons olive oil
1   cup water
⅔   cup loosely packed snipped fresh basil or 2 tablespoons dried basil, crushed
½   cup tomato paste
2   tablespoons red wine vinegar
8   ounces hot cooked pasta, such as penne, cavatelli, or tortellini
    Grated Parmesan cheese (optional)

1 For sauce, in a large skillet cook sweet peppers and garlic in hot oil over medium heat for 20 minutes, stirring occasionally. (Or, if using peppers from a jar, in a 2-quart saucepan cook garlic in hot oil for 3 to 4 minutes or until light brown; then add peppers.)

2 Place half of the pepper mixture in a blender container or food processor bowl. Cover; blend or process until nearly smooth. Add half each of the water, basil, tomato paste, and vinegar. Cover and blend or process with several on-and-off turns until basil is just chopped and mixture is nearly smooth. Transfer to a 2-quart saucepan. Repeat with remaining pepper mixture, water, basil, tomato paste, and vinegar; transfer to the saucepan.

3 Cook and stir sauce over medium heat until heated through. Serve sauce over hot pasta. If desired, sprinkle with Parmesan cheese.

Nutrition Facts per serving: 332 cal., 8 g total fat (1 g sat. fat), 0 mg chol., 48 mg sodium, 57 g carbo., 3 g fiber, 10 g pro.
Daily Values: 92% vit. A, 33% vit. C, 21% iron
Exchanges: 2 Vegetable, 3 Starch, 1 Fat

fresh herb substitutions

The use of fresh herbs is one of the hallmarks of fresh-tasting, flavorful cooking. Although each herb has its own distinctive flavor, there's no culinary rule that says you can't substitute one for another. Here are some fresh herb alternates to try:

- **Sage:** savory, marjoram, rosemary
- **Basil:** oregano, thyme
- **Thyme:** basil, marjoram, oregano, savory
- **Mint:** basil, marjoram, rosemary
- **Rosemary:** thyme, tarragon, savory
- **Cilantro:** parsley

Lasagna with Zucchini and Walnuts

The challenge of meatless lasagna is to make it as satisfying as the beef- or sausage-layered classic. Crunchy walnuts stand in for the meat, adding heartiness and texture.

Prep: 35 minutes **Bake:** 40 minutes **Stand:** 15 minutes **Makes:** 6 servings

- 2 medium zucchini
- 4 teaspoons olive oil
- 2 cups finely chopped onions
- 2 large carrots, finely chopped
- 4 cloves garlic, minced
- 2 cups purchased marinara sauce
- 1 tablespoon snipped fresh basil or 1 teaspoon dried basil, crushed
- 1/8 teaspoon black pepper
- 1 1/2 cups shredded mozzarella cheese (6 ounces)
- 1/2 cup grated Parmesan cheese
- 6 no-boil lasagna noodles*
- 1/2 cup chopped walnuts

1 Trim ends from zucchini. Cut zucchini lengthwise into 1/8-inch slices. Place in a single layer on a lightly greased baking sheet; brush with 1 teaspoon of the oil. Broil 3 to 4 inches from heat about 5 minutes or until crisp-tender, turning once. Let zucchini cool before handling.

2 In a large saucepan heat the remaining oil over medium-high heat. Add onions, carrots, and garlic; cook and stir about 5 minutes or until tender. Add marinara sauce, basil, and pepper. Bring to boiling; reduce heat. Simmer, covered, for 10 minutes, stirring occasionally. In a small bowl toss together the mozzarella and Parmesan cheeses. Reserve one-third of cheese for top; set cheese aside.

3 Grease a 2-quart square baking dish; arrange two noodles in the dish. Spread with one-third of the sauce. Sprinkle with one-third of the nuts. Top with one-third of the zucchini; sprinkle with one-third of the cheese mixture. Repeat layering, alternating strips of zucchini lengthwise and crosswise in each layer and ending with the zucchini.

4 Bake, covered, in a 375° oven for 20 minutes. Uncover and sprinkle with reserved cheese. Bake, uncovered, about 20 minutes more or until heated through. Let stand for 15 minutes before serving. If desired, sprinkle with additional chopped walnuts.

Nutrition Facts per serving: 358 cal., 19 g total fat (6 g sat. fat), 23 mg chol., 839 mg sodium, 33 g carbo., 3 g fiber, 17 g pro.
Daily Values: 100% vit. A, 28% vit. C, 29% calcium, 12% iron
Exchanges: 4 Vegetable, 1 Starch, 1 Medium-Fat Meat, 2 Fat

*Note: All brands of no-boil lasagna noodles are not the same size, so use enough noodles to make three even, single layers.

Teriyaki Penne ♥ FAST

Served over pasta tubes, this easy Asian stir-fry delivers a tasty bonus with every bite. The zippy ginger-spiked sauce coats the pasta inside and out for a double dose of flavor.

Start to finish: 25 minutes **Makes:** 4 servings

8 ounces dried tomato-basil penne or plain mostaccioli pasta

½ teaspoon grated fresh ginger

1 clove garlic, minced

1 tablespoon toasted sesame oil or cooking oil

3 cups packaged shredded broccoli (broccoli slaw mix)

2 cups sliced fresh mushrooms

¼ cup teriyaki sauce

¼ cup thinly sliced green onions

1 Cook pasta according to package directions; drain. Return pasta to saucepan.

2 Meanwhile, in a large skillet cook ginger and garlic in hot oil for 15 seconds. Stir in the shredded broccoli, mushrooms, and teriyaki sauce. Cook and stir about 5 minutes or until broccoli is crisp-tender.

3 To serve, toss broccoli mixture and green onions with hot pasta.

Nutrition Facts per serving: 286 cal., 5 g total fat (1 g sat. fat), 0 mg chol., 749 mg sodium, 50 g carbo., 5 g fiber, 11 g pro.
Daily Values: 14% vit. A, 72% vit. C, 3% calcium, 23% iron
Exchanges: 2½ Starch, 2 Vegetable, ½ Fat

Lo Mein with Tofu ♥ FAST

Look for soba noodles, a type of Japanese pasta made from buckwheat flour, at Asian specialty markets or in the Asian food section of your supermarket.

Start to finish: 25 minutes **Makes:** 4 servings

2 cups broccoli florets
1 cup thinly sliced carrots
4 ounces extra-firm light tofu (fresh bean curd), cut into ½-inch cubes
1 cup cold water
2 tablespoons reduced-sodium soy sauce
4 teaspoons cornstarch
½ teaspoon instant vegetable bouillon granules
8 ounces soba noodles (buckwheat noodles) or dried spaghetti
    Nonstick cooking spray
1 teaspoon toasted sesame oil
1 cup thinly sliced fresh mushrooms
4 large green onions, cut into ½-inch pieces
2 teaspoons grated ginger
2 cloves garlic, minced
1 tablespoon olive oil or cooking oil
2 teaspoons sesame seeds, toasted

1 In a covered medium saucepan cook the broccoli and carrots in a small amount of boiling water for 3 to 4 minutes or until crisp-tender; drain. Set vegetables aside. Pat the tofu dry with paper towels. In a small bowl stir together the cold water, soy sauce, cornstarch, and bouillon granules; set aside.

2 Cook noodles according to package directions until tender but still firm, except omit any oil or salt. Drain and keep warm.

3 Coat a cold nonstick wok or large skillet with cooking spray. Add ½ teaspoon of the sesame oil; heat over medium-high heat. Add the mushrooms, green onions, ginger, and garlic. Stir-fry for 1 to 2 minutes or until vegetables are crisp-tender. Remove vegetables. Add the olive oil and remaining sesame oil to the wok. Add the tofu; stir-fry for 1 to 2 minutes or just until tofu starts to brown. Remove the tofu. Add the broccoli-carrot mixture and mushroom mixture to the wok; push vegetables from center of the wok. Stir the soy sauce mixture; add to center of wok. Cook and stir until thickened and bubbly.

4 Add the noodles to the wok. Using 2 spatulas or forks, lightly toss the mixture for 3 to 4 minutes or until noodles are heated through. Add the tofu; toss lightly. Cover; cook for 1 to 2 minutes or until heated through. Sprinkle with sesame seeds; serve immediately.

Nutrition Facts per serving: 241 cal., 5 g total fat (1 g sat. fat), 0 mg chol., 704 mg sodium, 43 g carbo., 3 g fiber, 10 g pro.
Daily Values: 74% vit. A, 40% vit. C, 4% calcium, 15% iron
Exchanges: 2 Vegetable, 2 Starch, 1 Fat

Oven-Roasted Vegetable Pasta

Meat lovers usually have to wait hours to experience the mellow, caramelized sweetness of their favorite roasts. This recipe brings these irresistible qualities to vegetables in much less time.

Prep: 15 minutes **Roast:** 30 minutes **Makes:** 4 servings

9   medium plum tomatoes, cored and sliced ¼ inch thick
2   medium zucchini, halved lengthwise and sliced ½ inch thick
2   tablespoons olive oil
4   cloves garlic, minced
½   teaspoon salt
¼   teaspoon black pepper
6   ounces dried penne or rotini pasta
3   tablespoons Italian-style tomato paste
½   cup finely shredded Parmesan cheese (2 ounces)
¼   cup finely shredded fresh basil

1 Place tomatoes and zucchini in a 3-quart rectangular baking dish. In a small bowl combine olive oil, garlic, salt, and pepper; drizzle over tomato mixture. Roast vegetables, uncovered, in a 400° oven for 20 minutes, stirring once.

2 Meanwhile, cook pasta according to package directions; drain. Stir pasta and tomato paste into the roasted vegetable mixture. Bake, uncovered, for 10 minutes more.

3 Stir pasta and vegetable mixture before serving; sprinkle with Parmesan cheese and basil.

Nutrition Facts per serving: 344 cal., 13 g total fat (4 g sat. fat), 11 mg chol., 682 mg sodium, 46 g carbo., 5 g fiber, 14 g pro.
Daily Values: 17% vit. A, 66% vit. C, 23% calcium, 16% iron
Exchanges: 3 Vegetable, 2 Starch, 1 Lean Meat, 1½ Fat

Orzo with Root Vegetables ♥ FAST

When you're looking for a quick, light supper, enjoy this multi-hued dish. It's a little like a veggie-packed rice pilaf; because it's made with orzo (a rice-shaped pasta), it cooks up much quicker.

Start to finish: 30 minutes **Makes:** 4 servings

1 large onion, halved and
    thinly sliced
2 cloves garlic, minced
1 tablespoon olive oil
1¾ cups Vegetable Stock
    (recipe, page 18) or
    one 14½-ounce can
    vegetable broth
¼ cup water
½ teaspoon dried thyme,
    crushed
⅛ teaspoon ground red
    pepper
¾ cup orzo (rosamarina)
2 medium carrots, cut into
    thin strips
1 medium turnip, cut into
    thin strips
1 medium red sweet pepper,
    cut into thin strips
1 15-ounce can red beans,
    rinsed and drained

1 In a large saucepan cook onion and garlic in hot oil just until tender. Stir in stock, water, thyme, and ground red pepper. Bring to boiling. Stir in orzo and carrots. Simmer, covered, for 10 minutes.

2 Stir turnip, sweet pepper, and red beans into orzo mixture; return to boiling. Simmer, covered, for 2 to 3 minutes more or until orzo is tender.

Nutrition Facts per serving: 329 cal., 5 g total fat (1 g sat. fat), 5 mg chol., 335 mg sodium, 59 g carbo., 10 g fiber, 14 g pro.
Daily Values: 82% vit. A, 57% vit. C, 7% calcium, 29% iron
Exchanges: 2 Vegetable, 3 Starch, ½ Lean Meat

crushing dried herbs

You'll get more flavor out of dried herbs if you crush them before adding them to recipes.

For the correct amount of herb, first measure it in a measuring spoon, then empty the spoon into your hand. Crush the herb with the fingers of your other hand to release the herb's flavor, and add it to the specified ingredients.

Some dried herbs, such as rosemary and thyme, are more easily crushed with a mortar and pestle—but if you don't have one, try crushing them with a wooden spoon against the inside of a bowl. This is not an ideal substitute for a mortar and pestle but should do in a pinch.

Campanelle with Asiago Sauce

Break out the stylish tableware for this exquisite dish! Nutty Asiago cheese and a flower-shaped pasta make this dish a winning choice for enjoying with friends.

Prep: 20 minutes **Cook:** 12 minutes **Makes:** 4 servings

8 ounces dried campanelle
   (bell flower pasta) or
   penne pasta
2 small zucchini and/or
   yellow summer squash,
   halved lengthwise and
   sliced
½ cup snipped dried
   tomatoes, cut into strips
2 cloves garlic, minced
¼ cup dry white wine
¼ cup vegetable broth
2 tablespoons half-and-half
   or light cream
¾ cup grated Asiago cheese
¼ cup coarsely chopped
   hazelnuts, toasted
2 tablespoons snipped fresh
   Italian parsley
¼ teaspoon coarsely ground
   black pepper

1 In a Dutch oven cook pasta according to package directions, except add zucchini during the last 3 minutes of cooking. Drain; return mixture to pan.

2 Meanwhile, in a small saucepan combine the tomatoes, garlic, wine, and broth. Bring to boiling; reduce heat. Simmer, uncovered, about 3 minutes or until tomatoes are softened. Stir in half-and-half; heat through.

3 Add tomato mixture, cheese, nuts, 1 tablespoon of the parsley, and the pepper to pasta mixture. Toss to coat. Sprinkle with remaining parsley.

Nutrition Facts per serving: 410 cal., 16 g total fat (6 g sat. fat), 25 mg chol., 441 mg sodium, 51 g carbo., 4 g fiber, 16 g pro.
Daily Values: 8% vit. A, 18% vit. C, 23% calcium, 17% iron
Exchanges: 1 Vegetable, 3 Starch, 1 Medium-Fat Meat, 1½ Fat

Trattoria-Style Fettuccine ♥ FAST

This fettuccine special is just the kind of soulful pasta dish that neighborhood trattorias take pride in serving. It tosses an intensely flavored double-tomato sauce with tangy feta cheese.

Start to finish: 20 minutes **Makes:** 4 servings

1 9-ounce package refrigerated spinach fettuccine

2 tablespoons chopped shallots or onion

1 medium carrot, coarsely shredded (about ½ cup)

1 tablespoon olive oil

¼ cup oil-packed dried tomatoes, drained and snipped

4 medium (about 1¼ pounds) red and/or yellow tomatoes, coarsely chopped (about 2⅔ cups)

½ cup crumbled garlic and herb or peppercorn feta cheese (2 ounces)

1 Using kitchen scissors, cut the stack of fettuccine strands in half crosswise (for easier eating). Cook pasta according to package directions; drain. Return pasta to pan.

2 Meanwhile, in a large skillet cook shallots and carrot in hot oil over medium heat for 1 to 2 minutes or just until tender. Stir in dried and fresh tomatoes; cook for 1 to 2 minutes more or until heated through. Spoon tomato mixture over cooked pasta; toss gently. Sprinkle each serving with cheese.

Nutrition Facts per serving: 311 cal., 11 g total fat (3 g sat. fat), 72 mg chol., 243 mg sodium, 44 g carbo., 2 g fiber, 13 g pro.
Daily Values: 96% vit. A, 53% vit. C, 13% calcium, 20% iron
Exchanges: 3 Starch, ½ Medium-Fat Meat, 1 Fat

Skillet Pasta and Vegetables

Use your favorite combination of frozen vegetables. The cooking time is about the same for all varieties.

Start to finish: 50 minutes **Makes:** 6 servings

2 tablespoons olive oil
2 cloves garlic, minced
6 ½-inch slices baguette-style French bread
2¼ cups water
1 14-ounce jar chunky-style spaghetti sauce with mushrooms (about 1½ cups)
8 ounces dried wagon wheel pasta (about 2½ cups)
3 cups loose-pack frozen vegetables, such as white boiling onions, sugar snap peas, and cauliflower
2 teaspoons olive oil
¼ teaspoon salt
⅛ teaspoon black pepper
½ cup ricotta cheese
2 tablespoons milk
½ teaspoon dried oregano, crushed
¼ teaspoon black pepper
¾ cup shredded mozzarella cheese (3 ounces)
¼ cup grated Parmesan cheese

1 Combine the 2 tablespoons olive oil and the garlic. Brush both sides of bread slices with oil mixture. Place on a baking sheet and bake in a 400° oven for 4 minutes. Turn and bake for 4 to 5 minutes more or until bread is toasted. Set aside.

2 In a 10-inch skillet bring the water and spaghetti sauce to boiling; stir in uncooked pasta. Return to boiling; reduce heat. Simmer, covered, for 12 minutes, stirring pasta occasionally.

3 Meanwhile, place frozen vegetables in a colander; run cool water over the vegetables to thaw. Press with a rubber spatula to remove excess liquid. Transfer vegetables to a large bowl. Add the 2 teaspoons olive oil, salt, and pepper; toss mixture gently to coat. Set aside.

4 In a small bowl stir together ricotta cheese, milk, oregano, and the ¼ teaspoon black pepper. Stir in ½ cup of the mozzarella cheese and the Parmesan cheese.

5 Spoon cheese mixture over the pasta mixture in the skillet; spread cheese mixture slightly to a 4- to 5-inch circle. Spoon vegetables evenly around edge of skillet over pasta mixture (do not cover cheese in center). Simmer, covered, about 10 minutes or until vegetables are crisp-tender.

6 To serve, sprinkle pasta-vegetable mixture with the remaining ¼ cup mozzarella cheese. Top each serving with a bread slice.

Nutrition Facts per serving: 483 cal., 17 g total fat (6 g sat. fat), 22 mg chol., 845 mg sodium, 65 g carbo., 5 g fiber, 18 g pro.
Daily Values: 24% vit. A, 35% vit. C, 28% calcium, 18% iron
Exchanges: 2 Vegetable, 3½ Starch, 1 Medium-Fat Meat, 2 Fat

Pasta with Squash and Asparagus

Butternut squash, asparagus, and fresh mushrooms combine for a wonderfully varied, enticingly unexpected dish that's as creamy and sophisticated as a fine northern Italian specialty.

Prep: 25 minutes **Cook:** 10 minutes **Makes:** 4 servings

3 cups sliced shiitake
mushrooms, chanterelle
mushrooms, and/or
other fresh mushrooms

2 cloves garlic, minced

1 tablespoon snipped fresh
rosemary or 1 teaspoon
dried rosemary, crushed

1 tablespoon olive oil

⅓ cup dry white wine

⅓ cup vegetable broth

⅓ cup whipping cream

¼ teaspoon salt

8 ounces dried bow tie pasta

1 1-pound butternut squash,
peeled, seeded, and cut
into ½-inch pieces
(about 2 cups)

8 ounces asparagus, trimmed
and cut into 2-inch
pieces (about 1½ cups)

⅓ cup finely shredded
Parmesan cheese

1 In a large skillet cook and stir mushrooms, garlic, and rosemary in hot oil over medium heat for 4 to 5 minutes or until mushrooms are tender. Stir in wine, broth, whipping cream, and salt. Bring to boiling; reduce heat. Simmer, uncovered, about 4 minutes or until sauce is the consistency of light cream and is reduced to 1½ cups; set aside.

2 Meanwhile, in a large Dutch oven cook pasta according to package directions, except add squash during the last 7 minutes of cooking. Add asparagus during last 2 minutes of cooking. Drain. Return pasta mixture to Dutch oven. Add mushroom mixture and Parmesan cheese; toss to coat.

Nutrition Facts per serving: 479 cal., 16 g total fat (7 g sat. fat), 89 mg chol., 354 mg sodium, 70 g carbo., 4 g fiber, 15 g pro.
Daily Values: 151% vit. A, 43% vit. C, 17% calcium, 19% iron
Exchanges: 2 Vegetable, 4 Starch, 1 Medium-Fat Meat, 1½ Fat

Stuffed Shells with Fennel

Only in recent years have fennel bulbs become mainstream enough to appear regularly in produce aisles. Make up for lost time by enjoying the vegetable's subtle licorice-like flavor in this satisfying dish.

Prep: 40 minutes **Bake:** 35 minutes **Makes:** 5 servings

15   dried jumbo pasta shells
1   large onion, chopped
       (1 cup)
1   small bulb fennel,
       trimmed and chopped
       (1 cup)
2   cloves garlic, minced
2   tablespoons olive oil
1½   cups chopped broccoli
¼   cup water
1   cup part-skim ricotta
       cheese
⅓   cup finely shredded
       pecorino Romano cheese
1   tablespoon snipped fresh
       basil
    Nonstick cooking spray
1   26-ounce jar marinara
       sauce
¼   cup dry red wine
       (optional)
1½   teaspoons fennel seeds,
       crushed
    Finely shredded
       pecorino Romano
       cheese (optional)

1 Cook pasta according to package directions. Drain; rinse with cold water. Drain again; set aside.

2 In a large skillet cook onion, fennel, and garlic in hot oil until onion is tender. Add broccoli and water. Cook, covered, over medium-low heat for 4 to 5 minutes or just until vegetables are tender. Remove from heat; drain. Stir in ricotta cheese, pecorino Romano cheese, and basil.

3 Lightly coat a 2-quart rectangular baking dish with cooking spray. Spread ½ cup of the marinara sauce in the dish. Spoon cheese mixture into cooked pasta shells. Arrange stuffed shells in dish.

4 Combine remaining marinara sauce, wine (if desired), and fennel seeds; spoon over stuffed shells. Cover dish loosely with foil. Bake in a 375° oven for 35 minutes or until heated through. If desired, sprinkle with additional cheese.

Nutrition Facts per serving: 324 cal., 13 g total fat (4 g sat. fat), 19 mg chol., 792 mg sodium, 40 g carbo., 9 g fiber, 13 g pro.
Daily Values: 12% vit. A, 78% vit. C, 29% calcium, 13% iron
Exchanges: 2 Vegetable, 2 Starch, ½ Medium-Fat Meat, 1½ Fat

Summertime Eggplant and Herbs

If you don't have ziti or bow tie pasta on hand, substitute any small to medium pasta, such as rotelle, gemelli, rigatoni, or penne.

Start to finish: 35 minutes **Makes:** 6 to 8 servings

6 ounces dried ziti or bow tie pasta
1 medium eggplant, peeled and chopped
¼ cup chopped onion
2 cloves garlic, minced
2 tablespoons olive oil
2 cups chopped tomatoes
1 cup cherry tomatoes, halved
¼ cup finely shredded fresh basil
1 tablespoon snipped fresh savory
¼ teaspoon salt
⅛ teaspoon black pepper
¼ cup finely shredded Parmesan or Romano cheese
2 tablespoons pine nuts or slivered almonds, toasted

1 Cook pasta according to package directions; drain. Meanwhile, in a large skillet cook and stir eggplant, onion, and garlic in hot oil until onion is tender. Stir in chopped tomatoes. Bring to boiling; reduce heat. Simmer, uncovered, for 5 minutes. Stir in the cherry tomatoes, basil, savory, salt, and pepper; heat through.

2 To serve, toss vegetable mixture with hot pasta. Sprinkle with Parmesan cheese and pine nuts.

Nutrition Facts per serving: 332 cal., 12 g total fat (3 g sat. fat), 6 mg chol., 92 mg sodium, 46 g carbo., 5 g fiber, 11 g pro.
Daily Values: 48% vit. C, 9% calcium, 16% iron
Exchanges: 3 Vegetable, 2 Starch, 2 High-Fat Meat

Pasta Rosa-Verde ♥ FAST

Head to the farmer's market for a basketful of fresh vegetables and herbs, then head home to prepare this recipe for vegetarian cooking at its freshest, quickest, and most colorful best.

Start to finish: 30 minutes **Makes:** 4 servings

8 ounces dried ziti or
   mostaccioli pasta
1 medium onion, thinly
   sliced
2 cloves garlic, minced
1 tablespoon olive oil
4 to 6 medium tomatoes,
   seeded and coarsely
   chopped (3 cups)
1 teaspoon salt
½ teaspoon freshly ground
   black pepper
¼ teaspoon crushed red
   pepper (optional)
3 cups arugula, watercress,
   and/or spinach, coarsely
   chopped
¼ cup pine nuts or slivered
   almonds, toasted
2 tablespoons crumbled
   Gorgonzola or other
   blue cheese

1 Cook pasta according to package directions. Drain; cover and keep warm. Meanwhile, in a large skillet cook onion and garlic in hot oil over medium heat until onion is tender. Add tomatoes, salt, black pepper, and, if desired, red pepper. Cook and stir over medium-high heat about 2 minutes or until the tomatoes are warm and release some of their juices.

2 Stir in arugula; heat just until greens are wilted. Top pasta with tomato mixture. Sprinkle with toasted nuts and cheese.

Nutrition Facts per serving: 352 cal., 11 g total fat (2 g sat. fat), 3 mg chol., 610 mg sodium, 54 g carbo., 2 g fiber, 12 g pro.
Daily Values: 12% vit. A, 41% vit. C, 6% calcium, 25% iron
Exchanges: 3 Vegetable, 2½ Starch, 1½ Fat

toasting nuts

Many nuts gain a flavor boost through toasting. As a general rule, to toast nuts, I spread them in a single layer in a shallow baking pan and bake them in a 350° oven for 5 to 10 minutes or until they're light golden brown. Watch them carefully and stir once or twice so they don't burn.

Marcellus Krantz

Test Kitchen Home Economist

Sandwiches & More

Sauteed Onion-Tomato Sandwiches

In this Chapter:

♥ Low-fat and no-fat recipes
* Fast recipes

Grilled Gazpacho Sandwiches ♥

Stay as cool as a cucumber with this hearty sandwich featuring the flavors of the cold soup gazpacho. Tomatoes and cucumbers are mixed with black beans, then scooped into grilled French bread "bowls."

Prep: 20 minutes **Grill:** 14 minutes **Makes:** 6 servings

1 medium cucumber, seeded and chopped
1 cup cooked or canned black beans, rinsed and drained
¼ cup snipped fresh cilantro
2 tablespoons cider vinegar
1 tablespoon olive oil
1 pickled jalapeño pepper, finely chopped
½ to 1 teaspoon chili powder
1 clove garlic, minced
 Salt and black pepper
3 large tomatoes, halved
1 large sweet onion (such as Vidalia or Walla Walla), cut into ½-inch slices
1 loaf French bread
1 cup shredded white cheddar or cheddar cheese (4 ounces)

1 In a medium bowl combine the cucumber, black beans, cilantro, vinegar, oil, jalapeño pepper, chili powder, and garlic. Season to taste with salt and black pepper. Set aside.

2 In a grill with a cover arrange medium coals in bottom of grill. Place tomatoes and onion on the lightly greased rack of grill directly over coals. Grill, uncovered, for 12 to 15 minutes or until vegetables are lightly charred, turning onion once halfway through grilling. Transfer vegetables to a cutting board; cool slightly. Coarsely chop vegetables; stir into the bean mixture.

3 Meanwhile, halve the French bread lengthwise. Cut each bread half crosswise into 3 pieces. Using a fork, hollow out the bread pieces slightly. Place bread pieces, cut sides down, on grill rack. Grill, uncovered, about 1 minute or until toasted. Remove from grill.

4 Spoon the bean mixture into the bread pieces; sprinkle with cheddar cheese. Return to grill. Cover and grill for 1 to 2 minutes or until cheese is melted.

Nutrition Facts per serving: 329 cal., 11 g total fat (5 g sat. fat), 20 mg chol., 634 mg sodium, 46 g carbo., 3 g fiber, 14 g pro.
Daily Values: 12% vit. A, 19% vit. C, 17% calcium, 18% iron
Exchanges: 1 Vegetable, 2½ Starch, 1 Medium-Fat Meat, ½ Fat

Peppery Artichoke Pitas ♥ FAST

Hungry and running on empty? Ten minutes is all it takes to make these creamy bean-and-artichoke-filled sandwiches.

Start to finish: 10 minutes **Makes:** 6 servings

1 15-ounce can Great Northern beans, rinsed and drained
1 14-ounce can artichoke hearts, drained and coarsely chopped
½ cup torn arugula or spinach
¼ cup bottled creamy garlic salad dressing
¼ teaspoon cracked black pepper
3 large pita bread rounds, halved crosswise

1 In a medium bowl combine the beans, artichoke hearts, arugula, salad dressing, and black pepper. To serve, spoon the bean mixture into pita bread halves.

Nutrition Facts per serving: 227 cal., 5 g total fat (1 g sat. fat), 3 mg chol., 269 mg sodium, 38 g carbo., 6 g fiber, 10 g pro.
Daily Values: 1% vit. A, 8% vit. C, 7% calcium, 16% iron
Exchanges: 1½ Vegetable, 2 Starch, ½ Fat

using arugula

Arugula is a peppery, pungent salad green with slender, deep green leaves. It adds a distinctive bite to salads or sandwiches. Wash it gently by immersing it in cold water several times to remove all traces of grit and sand. Pat dry with paper towels. Place the clean arugula in a plastic bag and refrigerate up to two days.

Eggplant Panini ♥ FAST

Why say sandwich when you can say panini? The Italian word sounds so much more enticing, with a promise of unexpected delights—even if it does simply mean bread roll in Italian!

Start to finish: 25 minutes **Makes:** 6 servings

1 cup torn arugula
2 teaspoons red wine vinegar
1 teaspoon olive oil
1/3 cup seasoned fine dry bread crumbs
2 tablespoons grated pecorino Romano or Parmesan cheese
1 egg
1 tablespoon milk
2 tablespoons all-purpose flour
1/2 teaspoon salt
1 medium eggplant, cut crosswise into 1/2-inch slices
1 tablespoon olive oil
3 ounces fresh mozzarella cheese, thinly sliced
1 12-inch plain or seasoned Italian flat bread (focaccia),* halved horizontally
1 large tomato, thinly sliced

1 In a small bowl toss together the arugula, vinegar, and the 1 teaspoon oil; set aside. In a shallow dish stir together the bread crumbs and Romano cheese. In another shallow dish beat together the egg and milk. In a third shallow dish stir together the flour and salt. Dip the eggplant slices into flour mixture to coat. Dip the slices into egg mixture, then coat both sides with crumb mixture.

2 In a 12-inch nonstick skillet heat the 1 tablespoon oil over medium heat. Add eggplant slices; cook for 6 to 8 minutes or until lightly browned, turning once. (Add more oil as necessary during cooking.) Top the eggplant with mozzarella cheese; reduce heat to low. Cook, covered, just until cheese begins to melt.

3 To serve, place the eggplant slices, cheese sides up, on bottom half of bread. Top with the arugula mixture, tomato slices, and top half of bread. Cut into wedges.

Nutrition Facts per serving: 318 cal., 10 g total fat (4 g sat. fat), 48 mg chol., 447 mg sodium, 45 g carbo., 5 g fiber, 13 g pro.
Daily Values: 10% vit. A, 11% vit. C, 18% calcium, 6% iron
Exchanges: 1 Vegetable, 2 1/2 Starch, 1 Medium-Fat Meat, 1/2 Fat

*Note: For easier slicing, purchase focaccia that is at least 2 1/2 inches thick.

Couscous Burritos ♥ FAST

Moroccan pasta in a Mexican burrito? Why not! Let this speedy international wrap rocket your taste buds in an entirely new direction.

Start to finish: 25 minutes **Makes:** 4 servings (8 burritos)

8 8-inch flavored or plain flour tortillas
1 cup Vegetable Stock (recipe, page 18) or vegetable broth
1 4½-ounce can diced green chile peppers, drained
¼ teaspoon ground turmeric
   Dash black pepper
⅔ cup quick-cooking couscous
¼ cup sliced green onions
1 cup chopped tomatoes
¾ cup chopped green sweet pepper
½ cup shredded reduced-fat taco cheese (2 ounces)
   Salsa (optional)

1 Wrap the tortillas in foil. Heat in a 350° oven about 10 minutes or until warm and soft. [Or, wrap tortillas in microwave-safe paper towels. Microwave on 100% power (high) for 30 seconds.]

2 Meanwhile, in a small saucepan combine the Vegetable Stock, chile peppers, turmeric, and black pepper. Bring to boiling; remove from heat. Stir in couscous and green onions. Cover and let stand for 5 minutes. Fluff with a fork. Stir in tomatoes and sweet pepper.

3 To assemble, spoon about ⅓ cup of the couscous mixture onto each tortilla just below center. Top with 1 tablespoon of the cheese. Roll up tortilla. If desired, serve burritos with salsa.

Nutrition Facts per serving: 359 cal., 8 g total fat (3 g sat. fat), 5 mg chol., 661 mg sodium, 60 g carbo., 7 g fiber, 13 g pro.
Daily Values: 10% vit. A, 97% vit. C, 16% calcium, 19% iron
Exchanges: 2 Vegetable, 3 Starch, ½ Medium-Fat Meat

Open-Face Portobello Sandwiches

Turn a familiar hors d'oeuvre—bread-stuffed mushrooms—upside down for a stunning open-face sandwich. Now it's bread on the bottom, mushrooms on top.

Start to finish: 25 minutes **Makes:** 4 servings

1 medium tomato, chopped
2 teaspoons snipped fresh basil, thyme, and/or oregano
⅛ teaspoon salt
2 medium fresh portobello mushrooms (about 4 inches in diameter)
1 teaspoon balsamic vinegar or red wine vinegar
½ teaspoon olive oil
½ of a 12-inch Italian flat bread (focaccia) or ½ of a 12-inch Italian bread shell (Boboli)
  Finely shredded Parmesan cheese (optional)

1 In a small bowl combine tomato, basil, and salt; set aside. Remove and discard stems from mushrooms. In a small bowl combine the vinegar and oil; gently brush over mushrooms.

2 Place mushrooms on the unheated rack of a broiler pan. Broil 4 to 5 inches from the heat for 6 to 8 minutes or just until mushrooms are tender, turning once halfway through broiling. (Or, grill on the rack of an uncovered grill directly over medium coals for 6 to 8 minutes, turning once halfway through grilling.) Drain mushrooms on paper towels. Thinly slice mushrooms; set aside.

3 Place the bread on a baking sheet. Broil for 2 to 3 minutes or until bread is heated through. (Or, place bread on grill rack. Grill for 2 to 3 minutes.)

4 To serve, arrange the mushroom slices and tomato mixture on top of bread. If desired, sprinkle with Parmesan cheese. Cut into wedges.

Nutrition Facts per serving: 161 cal., 3 g total fat (1 g sat. fat), 2 mg chol., 71 mg sodium, 29 g carbo., 3 g fiber, 7 g pro.
Daily Values: 1% vit. A, 15% vit. C, 4% calcium, 12% iron
Exchanges: 2 Vegetable, 1½ Starch

Grilled Sicilian-Style Pizza FAST

Sicilians like their escarole sauteed with lots of olive oil and served with chewy bread to sop up the juices. For maximum flavor in this grilled adaptation, use the tangy Italian cheese pecorino Romano.

Prep: 20 minutes **Grill:** 8 minutes **Makes:** 4 servings

1 large yellow or red tomato, thinly sliced

2 plum tomatoes, thinly sliced

4 ounces fresh mozzarella cheese, thinly sliced

⅓ cup halved pitted kalamata olives

1 12-inch Italian bread shell (Boboli)

1 tablespoon olive oil

1 cup coarsely chopped escarole or curly endive

¼ cup shredded pecorino Romano or Parmesan cheese

Freshly ground black pepper

1 Arrange the tomatoes, mozzarella cheese, and olives on top of bread. Drizzle with oil. Fold a 24×18-inch piece of heavy foil in half to make an 18×12-inch rectangle. Place the bread on foil, turning up ends of foil slightly.

2 In a grill with a cover arrange medium-hot coals around a drip pan. Test for medium heat above the pan. Place pizza on the grill rack over drip pan. Cover and grill about 8 minutes or until pizza is heated through, topping with escarole the last 2 minutes of grilling.

3 To serve, sprinkle the pizza with Romano cheese and freshly ground black pepper.

Nutrition Facts per serving: 459 cal., 19 g total fat (4 g sat. fat), 26 mg chol., 893 mg sodium, 54 g carbo., 3 g fiber, 24 g pro.
Daily Values: 12% vit. A, 14% vit. C, 31% calcium, 18% iron
Exchanges: 1 Vegetable, 3 Starch, 1½ Medium-Fat Meat, 1½ Fat

fresh is best

They may have the same last name, but the similarity ends there. Fresh mozzarella—made from whole milk—has a much softer texture and sweeter, more delicate flavor than regular mozzarella, which is made in reduced-fat and fat-free versions and is aged to give it a longer shelf life. Fresh mozzarella, usually packaged in whey or water and shaped into irregular balls, must be eaten within a few days of purchase. It's available in Italian markets, cheese shops, and increasingly, many supermarkets.

Sauteed Onion-Tomato Sandwiches

When laps double as the dining table, the best TV dinner is something easy and out-of-hand. This hearty whole-grain sandwich serves perfectly. Pass around beer, brownies, and your biggest napkins.

Start to finish: 20 minutes **Makes:** 4 servings

2   medium onions, sliced
1   teaspoon olive oil
8   slices hearty white, whole grain, or rye bread (toasted, if desired)
    Honey mustard
3   small red and/or yellow tomatoes, thinly sliced
4   lettuce leaves, shredded
    Small fresh basil leaves
4   ounces spreadable Brie cheese or tub-style cream cheese

1 In a large skillet cook onion slices in hot oil over medium-high heat for 5 to 7 minutes or until onions are tender and just starting to brown, stirring frequently. Remove from heat; cool slightly.

2 To assemble, lightly spread one side of 4 bread slices with honey mustard. Top with the onion slices, tomato slices, lettuce, and basil. Spread one side of the remaining 4 bread slices with Brie cheese. Place the bread slices, cheese sides down, on top of sandwiches.

Nutrition Facts per serving: 287 cal., 12 g total fat (6 g sat. fat), 28 mg chol., 490 mg sodium, 35 g carbo., 1 g fiber, 12 g pro.
Daily Values: 8% vit. A, 16% vit. C, 8% calcium, 15% iron
Exchanges: 1 Vegetable, 2 Starch, ½ Medium-Fat Meat, 1 Fat

Ginger Tofu Salad Wraps ♥

Tofu is cholesterol free and low in fat—but food-lovers shouldn't hold that against the humble, healthful ingredient! Here, it absorbs the great variety of nutty, spicy, and sour ingredients of the marinade.

Prep: 30 minutes **Marinate:** 30 minutes **Makes:** 4 servings (18 wraps)

1   12- to 14-ounce package firm or extra-firm tofu (fresh bean curd)
4   green onions, sliced
2   tablespoons reduced-sodium soy sauce
1   tablespoon rice vinegar
1   teaspoon toasted sesame oil
1   teaspoon grated fresh ginger
2   cloves garlic, minced
⅛   teaspoon ground red pepper
¼   cup finely chopped red sweet pepper
8   8-inch round rice papers
    Arugula leaves
    Soy sauce (optional)

1 If necessary, drain tofu. Cut into ½-inch cubes. Place the tofu and green onions in a medium bowl.

2 For marinade, in a screw-top jar combine the soy sauce, rice vinegar, sesame oil, ginger, garlic, and ground red pepper. Cover and shake well. Pour over tofu mixture; toss gently to coat. Cover and marinate at room temperature for 30 minutes. Gently stir in the red sweet pepper; set aside.

3 Meanwhile, quickly dip each rice paper in water and place between damp cotton dish towels. Let stand about 10 minutes to soften.

4 To assemble, remove one rice paper from between towels. Place some arugula leaves and about ⅓ cup of the tofu mixture on rice paper just below center. Roll up just enough to enclose filling. Fold 2 sides of rice paper over filling; continue rolling up. Repeat with the remaining rice papers, arugula, and tofu mixture.* If desired, serve with additional soy sauce.

Nutrition Facts per serving: 163 cal., 4 g total fat (1 g sat. fat), 0 mg chol., 306 mg sodium, 24 g carbo., 2 g fiber, 8 g pro.
Daily Values: 16% vit. A, 38% vit. C, 15% calcium, 11% iron
Exchanges: 1½ Starch, ½ Medium-Fat Meat

*Note: To make ahead, assemble the wraps, cover, and refrigerate up to 1 hour before serving.

Zucchini, Corn, and Potato Tacos FAST

A chopped potato adds a little heft to this meatless taco that's made even more satisfying with colorful veggies, tofu, and a sprinkling of cheese. If you like, pass salsa, sliced green onions, and sour cream.

Start to finish: 30 minutes **Makes:** 6 servings (12 tacos)

 1 medium potato, cut into
    ½-inch cubes (1 cup)
 2 medium carrots, chopped
12 taco shells
 1 tablespoon olive oil or
    cooking oil
½ cup chopped onion
 1 clove garlic, minced
 1 small zucchini, cut into
    thin bite-size strips
    (about 1¼ cups)
 1 cup cut fresh corn or
    frozen whole kernel
    corn
 1 tablespoon chili powder
½ teaspoon salt
⅛ teaspoon black pepper
 8 ounces firm tofu (fresh
    bean curd), cut into
    ½-inch cubes (1½ cups)
 1 cup shredded cheddar
    and/or Monterey Jack
    cheese (4 ounces)

1 In a covered medium saucepan cook the potato and carrots in a small amount of boiling water for 7 to 8 minutes or just until tender; drain and set aside. If desired, heat taco shells according to package directions.

2 Meanwhile, in a large skillet heat oil over medium-high heat. Add onion and garlic; cook and stir for 2 minutes. Add zucchini and corn; cook and stir for 3 minutes. Add chili powder, salt, and pepper; cook and stir for 1 minute more. Gently stir in the potato mixture and tofu; heat through.

3 To serve, fill the taco shells with vegetable mixture. Sprinkle with cheddar and/or Monterey Jack cheese.

Nutrition Facts per serving: 315 cal., 16 g total fat (5 g sat. fat), 20 mg chol., 438 mg sodium, 34 g carbo., 3 g fiber, 11 g pro.
Daily Values: 64% vit. A, 12% vit. C, 17% calcium, 14% iron
Exchanges: 1 Vegetable, 2 Starch, 1 Medium-Fat Meat, 1½ Fat

Falafel Burgers in Pitas FAST

In a traditional version of this hearty Middle Eastern specialty, the spicy bean patties are deep-fried; pan frying the patties is easier and cuts down considerably on the amount of oil needed.

Prep: 20 minutes **Cook:** 8 minutes **Makes:** 4 servings

¼ cup fine dry bread crumbs
1 15-ounce can garbanzo beans, rinsed and drained
½ cup chopped onion
2 cloves garlic, minced
1 teaspoon ground cumin
¼ cup snipped fresh parsley
2 tablespoons all-purpose flour
   Milk
1 tablespoon olive oil
2 large pita bread rounds, halved crosswise
½ of a small cucumber, thinly sliced
1 small tomato, thinly sliced
¼ cup bottled cucumber ranch or creamy cucumber salad dressing

1 Place the bread crumbs in a shallow dish; set aside. In a food processor bowl combine the garbanzo beans, onion, garlic, and cumin. Cover and process until mixture is coarsely ground. Stir in the parsley and flour.

2 Shape the bean mixture into four 3-inch-diameter patties. Carefully brush the patties with milk, then coat both sides with bread crumbs.

3 In a large nonstick skillet heat oil over medium heat. Add patties. Cook for 8 to 10 minutes or until patties are lightly browned, turning once. (Add more oil as necessary during cooking.)

4 To serve, fill the pita halves with the patties, cucumber, and tomato slices. Drizzle with salad dressing.

Nutrition Facts per serving: 337 cal., 13 g total fat (2 g sat. fat), 0 mg chol., 746 mg sodium, 45 g carbo., 7 g fiber, 10 g pro.
Daily Values: 19% vit. A, 29% vit. C, 11% calcium, 16% iron
Exchanges: 1 Vegetable, 2½ Starch, 2 Fat

INDEX

Photographs indicated in bold.

Metric Cooking Hints

By making a few conversions, cooks in Australia, Canada, and the United Kingdom can use the recipes in this book with confidence. The charts on this page provide a guide for converting measurements from the U.S. customary system, which is used throughout this book, to the imperial and metric systems. There also is a conversion table for oven temperatures to accommodate the differences in oven calibrations.

Product Differences: Most of the ingredients called for in the recipes in this book are available in English-speaking countries. However, some are known by different names. Here are some common U.S. American ingredients and their possible counterparts:

- Sugar is granulated or castor sugar.
- Powdered sugar is icing sugar.
- All-purpose flour is plain household flour or white flour. When self-rising flour is used in place of all-purpose flour in a recipe that calls for leavening, omit the leavening agent (baking soda or baking powder) and salt.
- Light-colored corn syrup is golden syrup.
- Cornstarch is cornflour.
- Baking soda is bicarbonate of soda.
- Vanilla is vanilla essence.
- Green, red, or yellow sweet peppers are capsicums.
- Golden raisins are sultanas.

Volume and Weight: U.S. Americans traditionally use cup measures for liquid and solid ingredients. The chart, above right, shows the approximate imperial and metric equivalents. If you are accustomed to weighing solid ingredients, the following approximate equivalents will help.

- 1 cup butter, castor sugar, or rice = 8 ounces = about 230 grams
- 1 cup flour = 4 ounces = about 115 grams
- 1 cup icing sugar = 5 ounces = about 140 grams

Spoon measures are used for smaller amounts of ingredients. Although the size of the tablespoon varies slightly in different countries, for practical purposes and for recipes in this book, a straight substitution is all that's necessary.

Measurements made using cups or spoons always should be level unless stated otherwise.

Equivalents: U.S. = U.K./Australia

⅛ teaspoon = 1 ml
¼ teaspoon = 1.25 ml
½ teaspoon = 2.5 ml
1 teaspoon = 5 ml
1 tablespoon = 15 ml
1 fluid ounce = 30 ml
¼ cup = 60 ml
⅓ cup = 80 ml
½ cup = 120 ml
⅔ cup = 160 ml
¾ cup = 180 ml
1 cup = 240 ml
2 cups = 475 ml
1 quart = 1 liter
½ inch = 1.25 cm
1 inch = 2.5 cm

Baking Pan Sizes

U.S.	Metric
8×1½-inch round baking pan	20×4-cm cake tin
9×1½-inch round baking pan	23×4-cm cake tin
11×7×1½-inch baking pan	28×18×4-cm baking tin
13×9×2-inch baking pan	32×23×5-cm baking tin
2-quart rectangular baking dish	28×18×4-cm baking tin
15×10×1-inch baking pan	38×25.5×2.5-cm baking tin (Swiss roll tin)
9-inch pie plate	22×4- or 23×4-cm pie plate
7- or 8-inch springform pan	18- or 20-cm springform or loose-bottom cake tin
9×5×3-inch loaf pan	23×13×8-cm or 2-pound narrow loaf tin or pâté tin
1½-quart casserole	1.5-liter casserole
2-quart casserole	2-liter casserole

Oven Temperature Equivalents

Fahrenheit Setting:	Celsius Setting*:	Gas Setting:
300°F	150°C	Gas Mark 2 (very low)
325°F	170°C	Gas Mark 3 (low)
350°F	180°C	Gas Mark 4 (moderate)
375°F	190°C	Gas Mark 5 (moderately hot)
400°F	200°C	Gas Mark 6 (hot)
425°F	220°C	Gas Mark 7 (hot)
450°F	230°C	Gas Mark 8 (very hot)
475°F	240°C	Gas Mark 9 (very hot)
Broil		Grill

*Electric and gas ovens may be calibrated using Celsius. However, for an electric oven, increase the Celsius setting 10 to 20 degrees when cooking above 160°C. For convection or forced-air ovens (gas or electric), lower the temperature setting 10°C when cooking at all heat levels.